ABANDONED VIRGINIA

VIRGINIA

THE FORGOTTEN COMMONWEALTH

JOEL HANDWERK

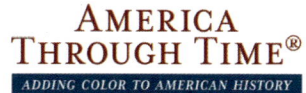

AMERICA
THROUGH TIME®
ADDING COLOR TO AMERICAN HISTORY

ABOUT THE AUTHOR

JOEL HANDWERK was born in Richmond, Virginia, and received his initial photography education at Clover Hill High School. It was here that he first learned 35mm film photography, including darkroom work, infrared photography, and night photography. In 2005 he received a college degree in Psychology from Asbury University. He enjoys photographing automobiles, cities at night, infrared landscapes, and occasionally dabbling in the retro practice of film photography. He lives in Richmond, Virginia, with his motorcycles and collection of film cameras.

America Through Time is an imprint of Fonthill Media LLC
www.through-time.com
office@through-time.com

Published by Arcadia Publishing by arrangement with Fonthill Media LLC
For all general information, please contact Arcadia Publishing:
Telephone: 843-853-2070
Fax: 843-853-0044
E-mail: sales@arcadiapublishing.com
For customer service and orders:
Toll-Free 1-888-313-2665

www.arcadiapublishing.com

First published 2021

ISBN 978-1-63499-295-4

Typeset in Trade Gothic 10pt on 15pt
Printed and bound in England

CONTENTS

About the Author   **2**

Introduction   **4**

1   St. Francis de Sales School   **5**

2   C&O Freight Receiving Depot   **15**

3   House in the Woods   **23**

4   Federated Paper Board Company Mill   **26**

5   Virginia Renaissance Faire   **31**

6   Southern Biscuit Company   **39**

7   Fulton Gas Works   **46**

8   Creighton Road Farmhouse   **56**

9   Central National Bank   **61**

10   Charles City Elementary   **72**

11   Jarratt School   **78**

12   Honeywell Warehouse   **83**

13   Union Level Ghost Town   **89**

Endnotes   **95**

INTRODUCTION

Several years ago, I read an online blog about a young woman who explored and photographed a disused Russian rocket factory. I was fascinated by her photos, and I soon discovered an entire online community of photographers who shared a passion for abandoned buildings. Even though I have yet to stumble upon any rocket factories, I have been fortunate enough to find a photogenic collection of vacant buildings in my home state of Virginia. Every one of these properties has a story behind it. Some were vacated decades ago, while others were vacated fairly recently. Some of these buildings have been destroyed since being photographed. Others have been renovated and put back to use again. But most of them are relatively unchanged, aside from being a little more weathered, or surrounded by taller undergrowth.

When exploring these buildings, I constantly have to remind myself that they were all brand new at one time. They had fresh paint, new furniture, and gleaming fixtures. A group of people were excited to start using the property, perhaps as a residence, a church, a bank, or even as a renaissance faire. These are all buildings that once started as the dream of a person, or of a collection of people, but now there is nothing left of those dreams. Perhaps the business closed, or the church moved on to a larger building, or any number of outcomes. As macabre as it sounds, this hobby has shown me that there is a fascinating component to the decay of something once wonderful. There is beauty to be found in the breakdown, if you know where to look.

1

ST. FRANCIS DE SALES SCHOOL

POWHATAN, VA

Sitting on a hill in Powhatan, the St. Francis de Sales School overlooks the James River. The school was often referred to as, "The Castle on the James," an apt description when considering the prominent towers and overall Gothic construction. The school was founded by Sister Katherine Drexel, the daughter of Francis Drexel, a wealthy banker with business ties to J. P. Morgan. Sister Katherine established the Sisters of the Blessed Sacrament in 1891, and she used her inheritance to support a total of sixty schools and missions during her lifetime. She built the St. Francis de Sales School as a high school for African American and Native American girls.[1]

Construction of the St. Francis de Sales School began in 1895, and was completed in 1899. Over the seventy-one years of its operation, the school has accumulated an alumnae population which exceeds 8,000. Attendees of the school were formally referred to as "Castleites." During a time in the American South when opportunities for African Americans were limited, this school was a welcome place for young girls to obtain a formal education. However, funding for the school became scarce after the death of Sister Katherine. The remainder of her inheritance reverted back to charities selected by her late father, in accordance with the conditions of his will. The institution ceased operation in 1970, and has not been used for schooling since closure.[2]

The St. Francis de Sales School is constructed in Gothic style, using over 500,000 red bricks that were sourced from local clay. These bricks were shaped and fired in a kiln located right on the construction site. There was a substantial renovation completed between 1952 and 1955, which added a four-story classroom building, aluminum replacement windows, and several modern upgrades to amenities.[3]

At the time when these photos were taken, the original stained-glass windows remained intact. After over 100 years since construction, it is nothing short of miraculous that these windows have survived. At the front of the chapel were three distinct altars, carved from Mexican onyx and Sienna marble.[4] Columns rose up the sides of the walls at intervals, and extended into arches which connect to the ceiling. This chapel was easily the most ornate place in the entire campus. Its deterioration was evident in the damaged plaster and missing ceiling panels. However, even in this state of partial decay, the building was impressive in the level of detail it possessed.

The structural integrity of this school appeared to be mostly intact. The worst interior breakdown in this building was limited to peeling paint, broken fixtures, and the chapel ceiling damages. However, there were some parts of the structure where entire walls were missing, or partially collapsed. There are also several places where rainwater is leaking into interior rooms. Signs of partial renovation were present, including construction materials and minor demolition.

After the school closed, a few of the Sisters remained at a historic house on the property, Belmead on the James, which is also owned by the Sisters of the Blessed Sacrament. They continued caring for both properties for decades. Some of these nuns lived in the Belmead house until as recently as 2017. At the time of writing, the property is for sale, with the hope that a buyer will attempt to restore the school building to its former condition.[5]

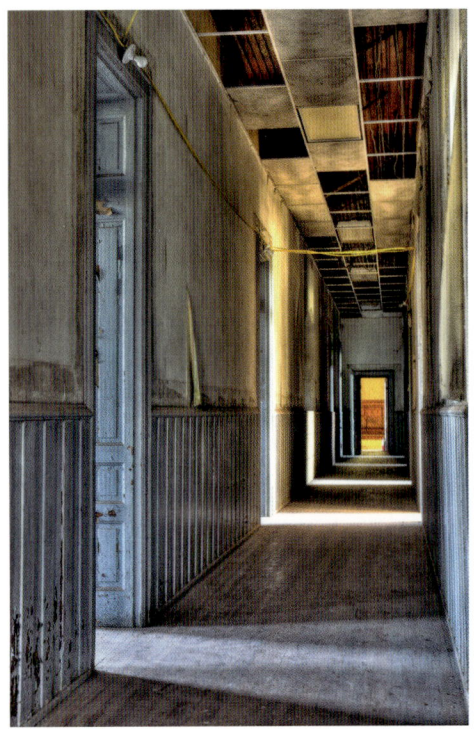

This is the main hallway for the ground floor, which felt noticeably colder than the rest of the building.

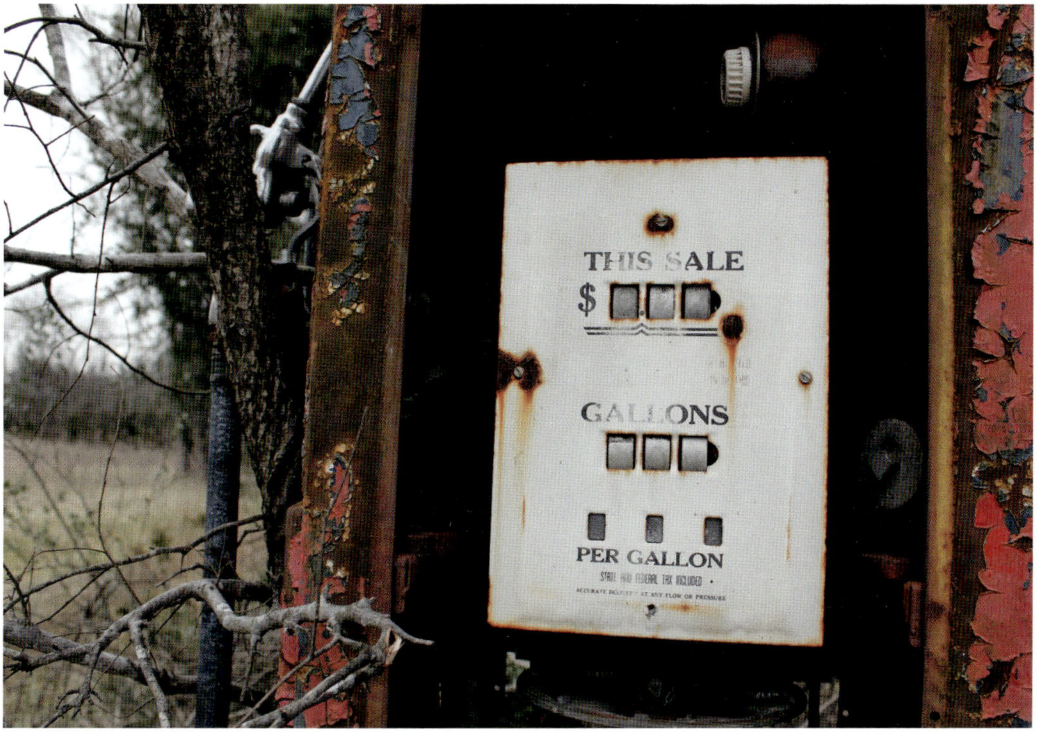

This fuel pump was located next to an outbuilding on the school grounds.

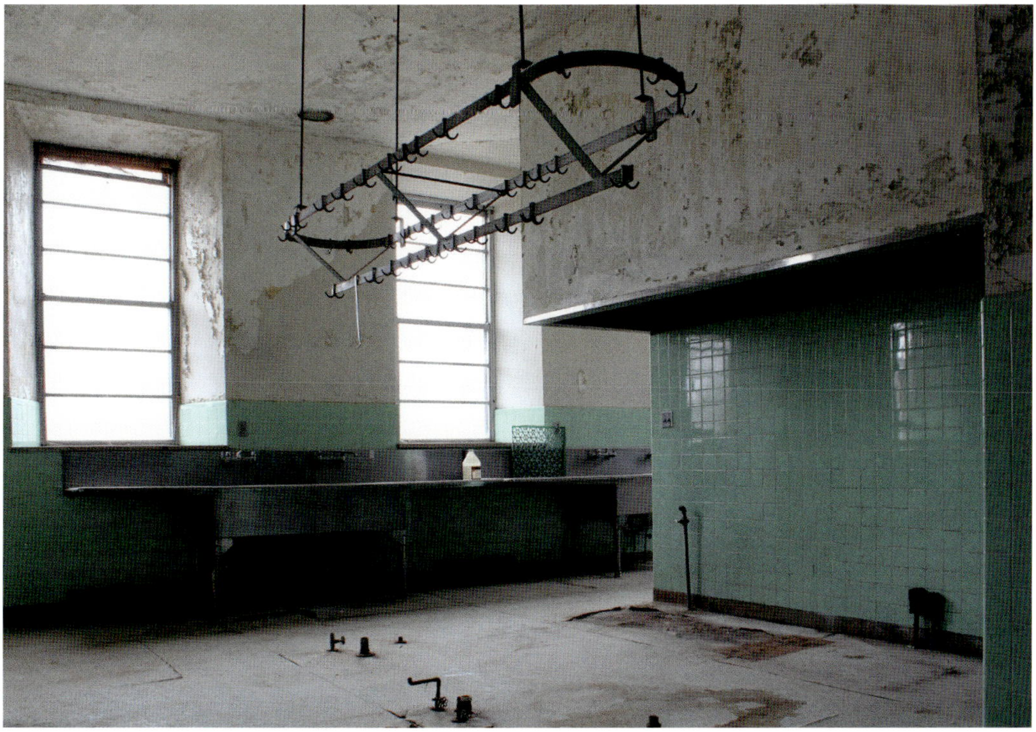

The former kitchen with some equipment removed from the floor.

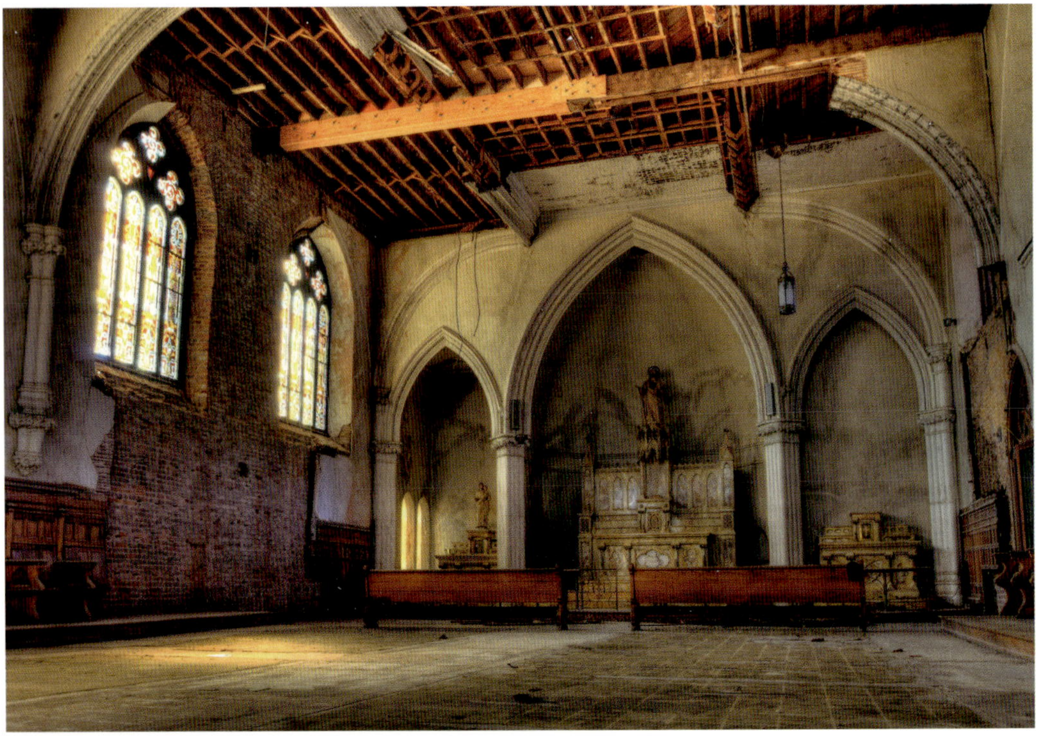

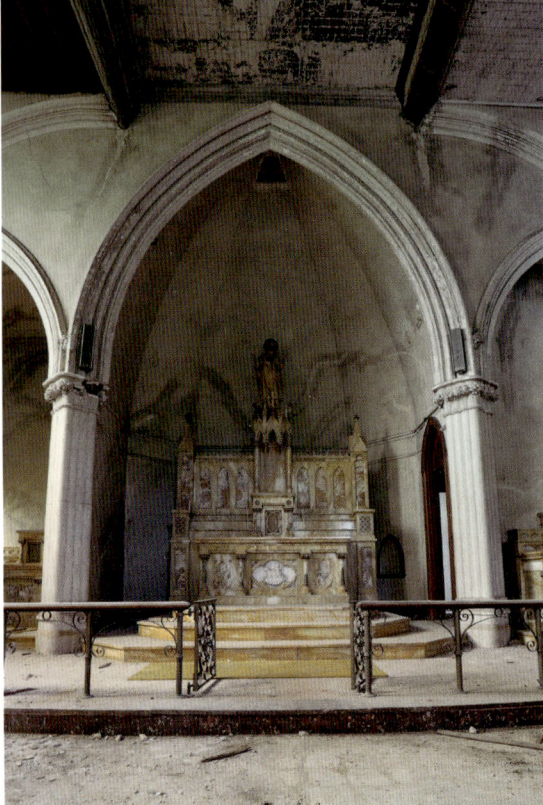

Above: A large chapel with pews removed and the ceiling under construction.

Left: The chapel altar was remarkably intact.

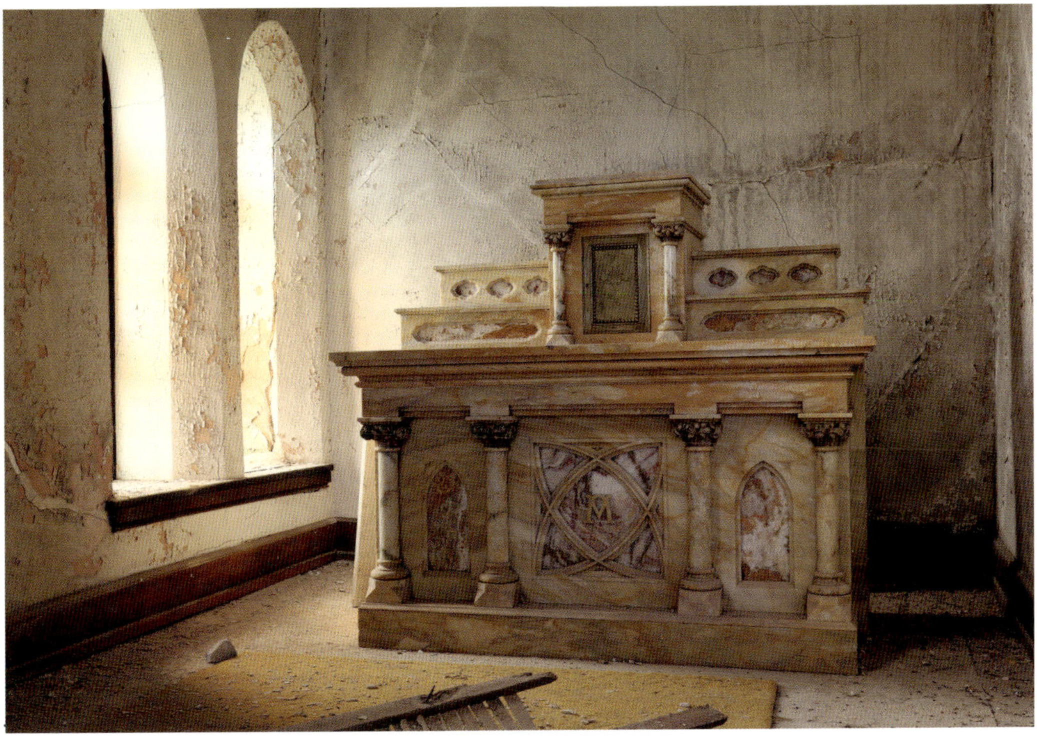

Above: This smaller marble altar sits on the left side of the central altar.

Right: A side door within the chapel, including elaborate detail on several surfaces.

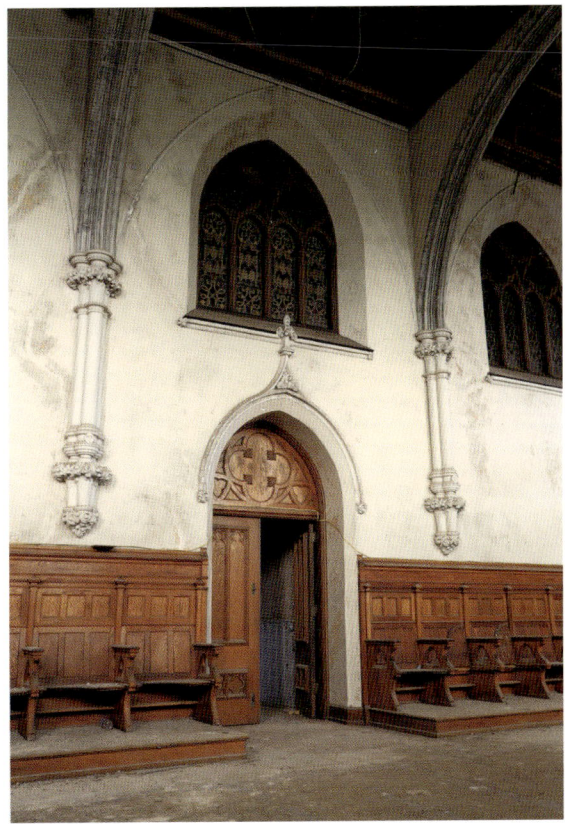

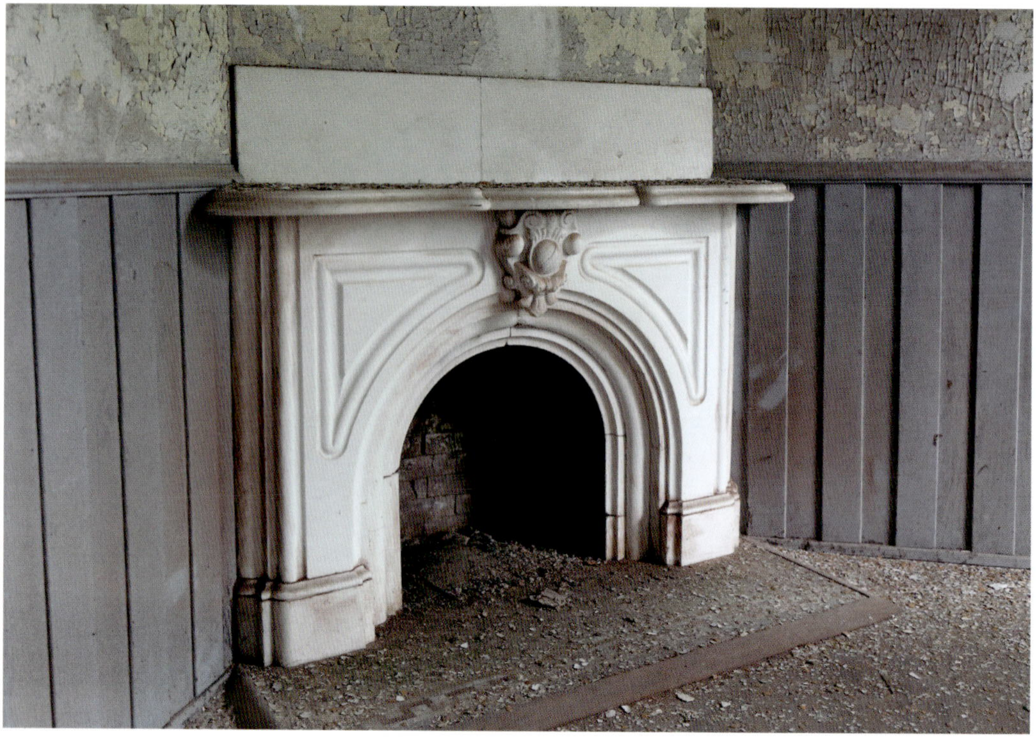

It's been decades since a fire burned in this fireplace.

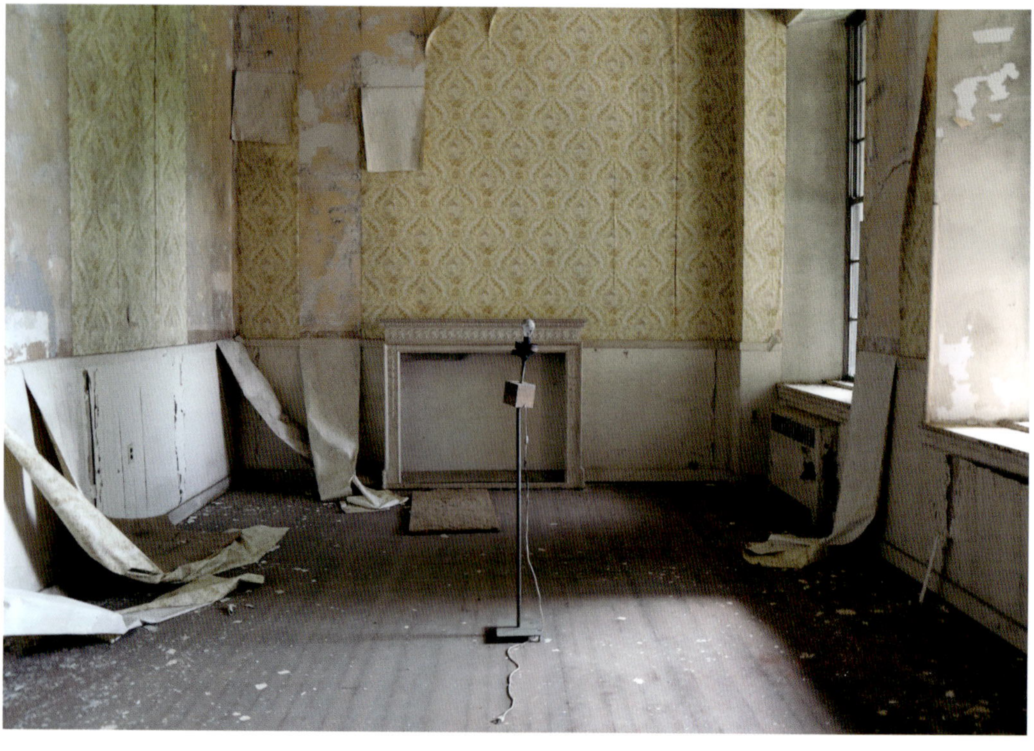

A lonely lightbulb stands among peeling wallpaper.

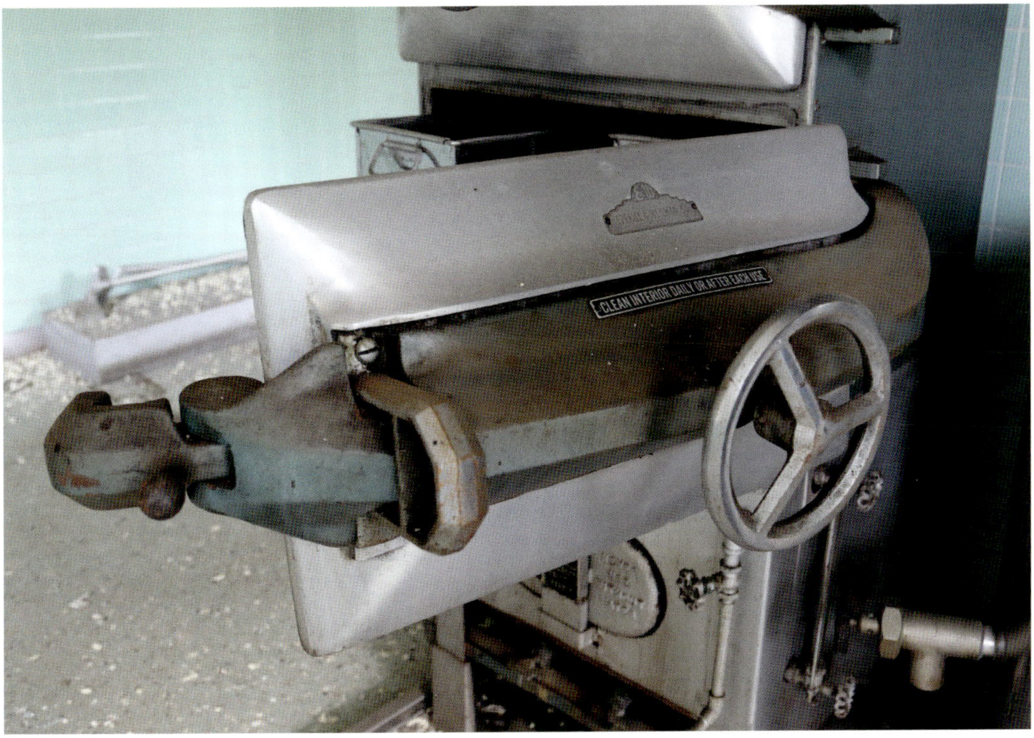

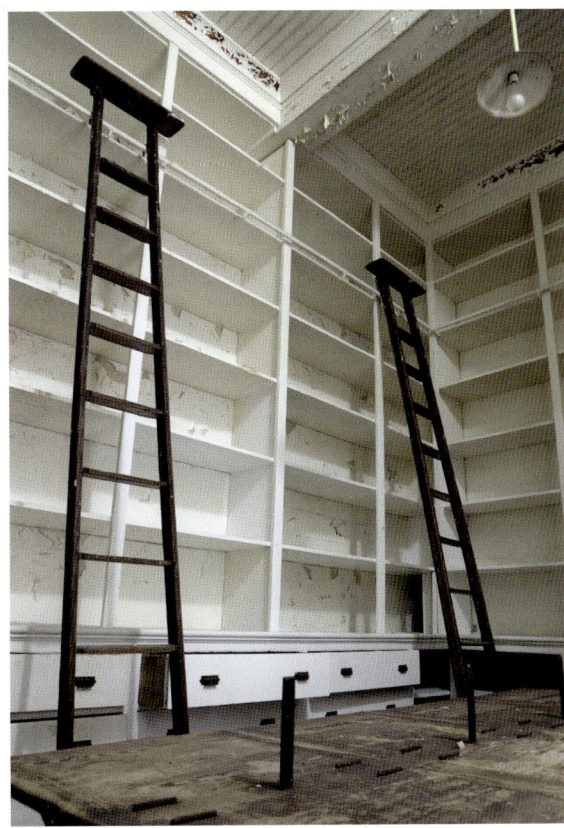

Above: A mostly intact boiler in the kitchen.

Right: This storage room has sliding ladders to improve ease of access to upper shelves.

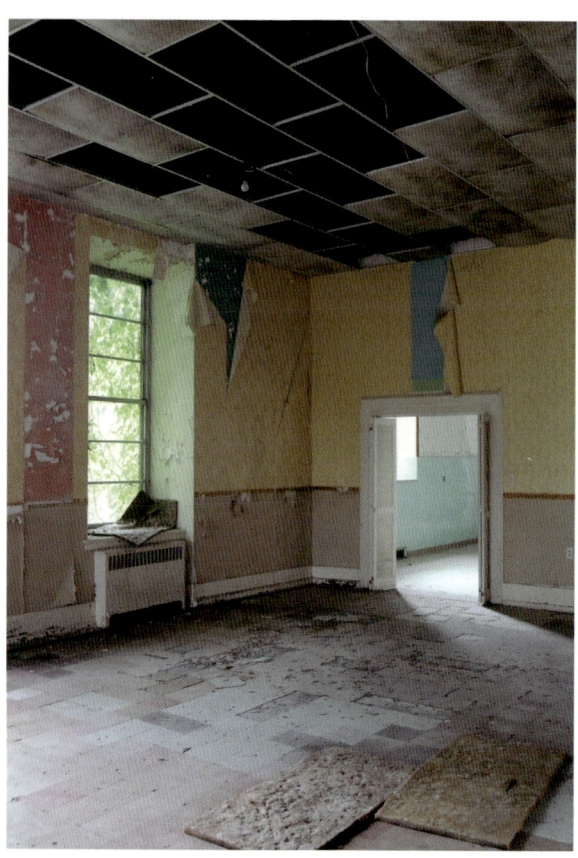

Below: Plastic chairs and peeling paint could be found throughout this room.

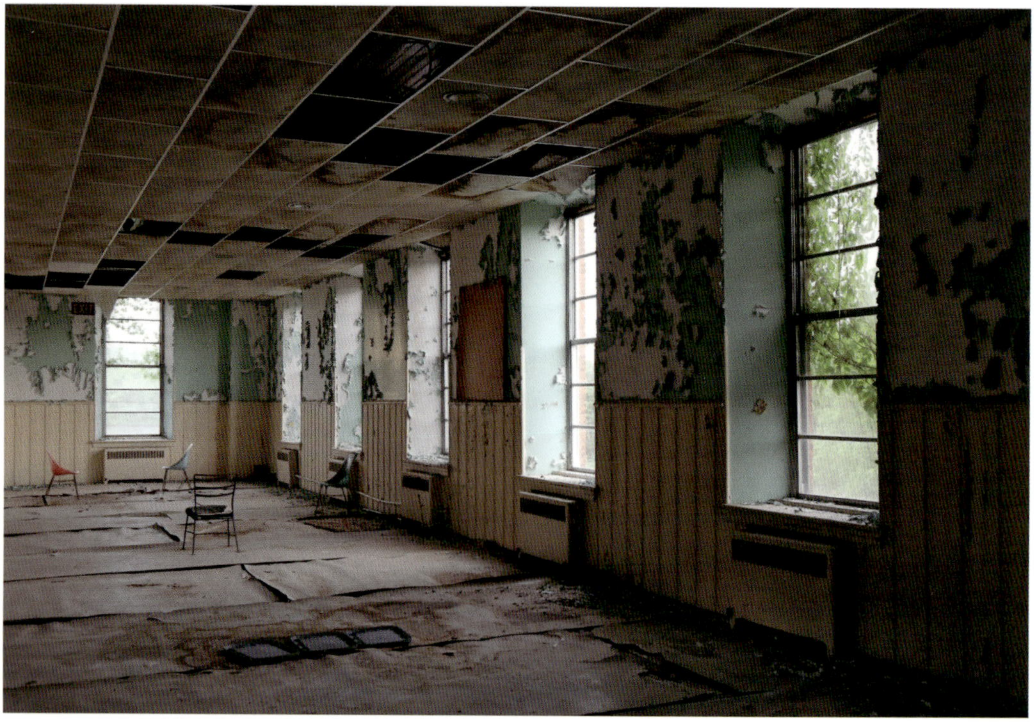

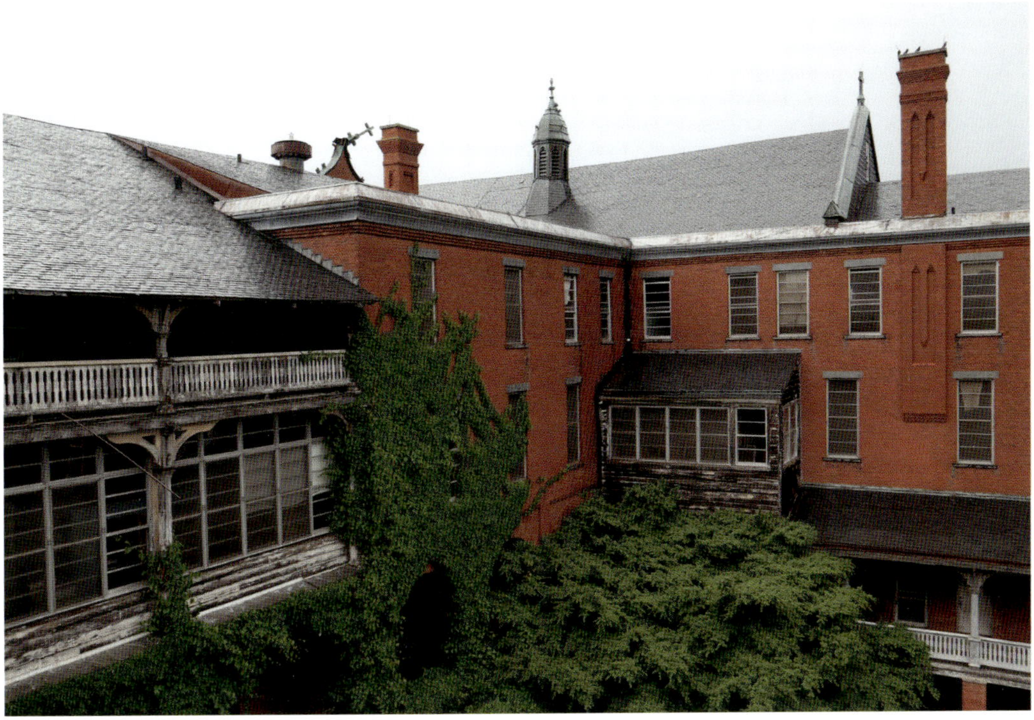

Above: Nature has already begun to reclaim this side of the building.

Right: A four-story staircase showing some signs of partial demolition.

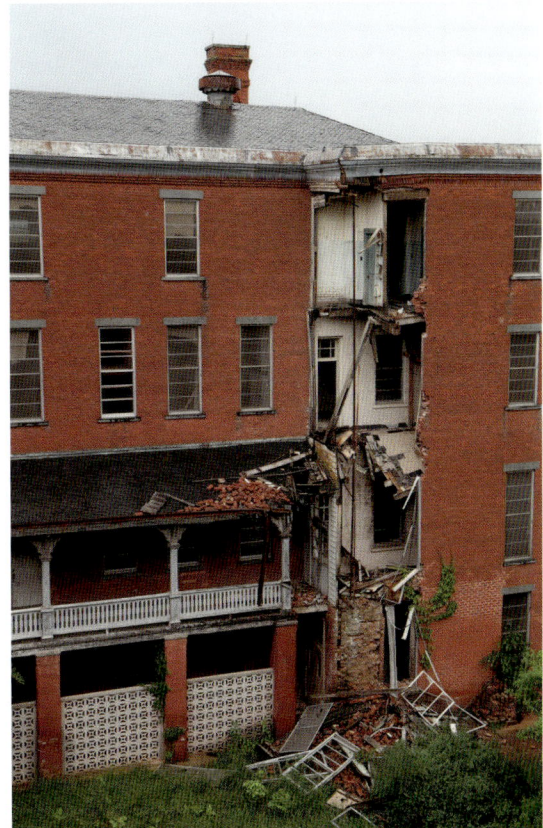

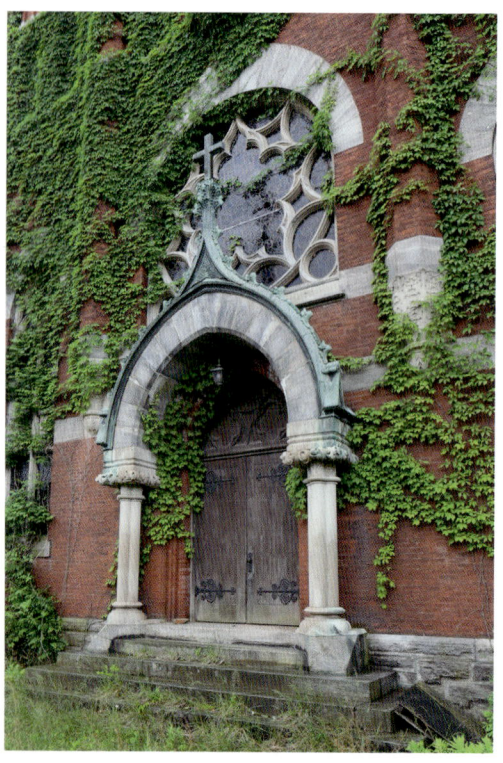

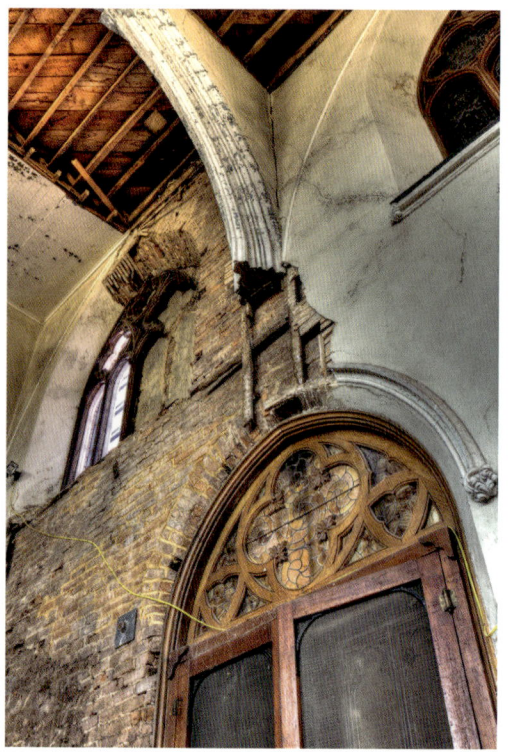

Ivy climbs the wall around the main entrance to the chapel.

More signs of decay inside the chapel.

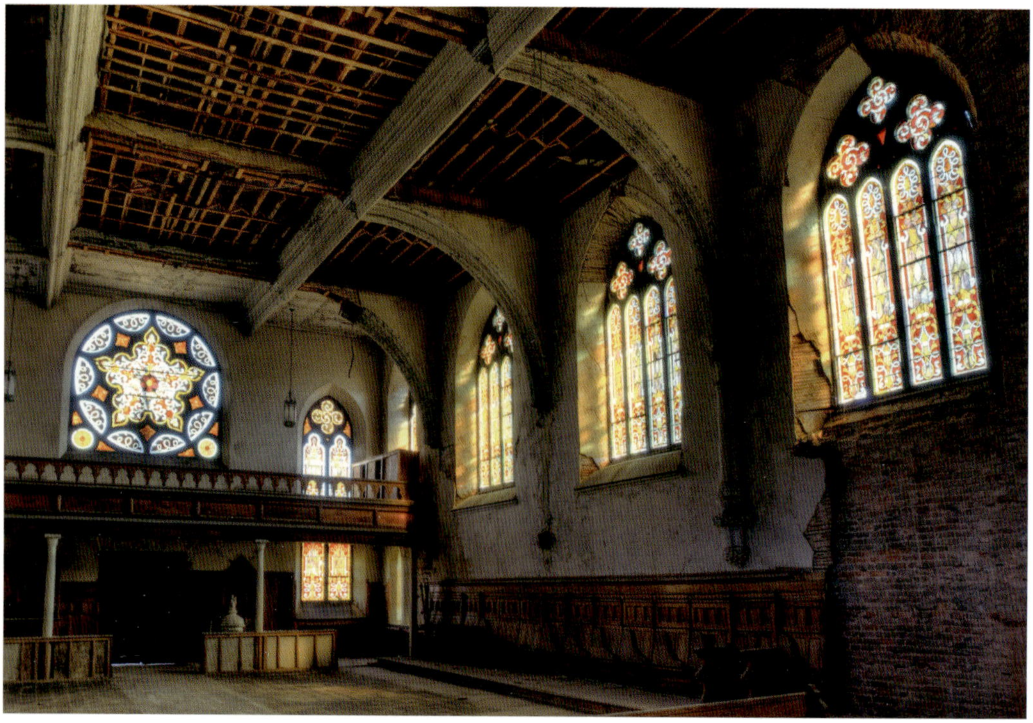

Stained-glass windows inside the chapel were undamaged.

2

C&O FREIGHT RECEIVING DEPOT

RICHMOND, VA

The Chesapeake & Ohio Railway (C&O) Freight Receiving Depot was located within the Shockoe Valley and Tobacco Row Historic District, in the heart of industrial Richmond. Just east of Interstate 95, this district represents Richmond's earliest manufacturing, residential, and commercial activity. After Richmond suffered significant damage during the Civil War, the rebuilding process was facilitated in part by the strength of the local tobacco industry. The Shockoe Valley and Tobacco Row Historic District was a central player in the recovery of the city during this post-bellum period.[1]

This railroad depot was constructed *circa* 1920, and was used as a storage facility for the C&O Railway. It was used primarily for commercial goods, and it is one of several railroad depots to have existed in this part of the city. The two-story building is constructed primarily of brick, with twenty exterior loading bays.[2] A few of these bays still featured large sliding wooden doors at the time when these photos were taken. I found evidence that the building was being used for shelter by the homeless population, which makes sense given that there were several unlocked exterior doors. This location was devoid of any spray-painting or other signs of vandalism. For an easily accessible property in the center of the city, this was rather unusual.

Even though it is unclear exactly when this facility ceased to be used as a railroad depot, it had likely been at least a few decades. During my visit, it appeared that the building was still being used for storage of some sort. This building contained a multifarious collection of objects, such as furniture, oil paintings, cassette tapes, construction materials, interior lamps, tools, stuffed animals, and even some dismembered pianos. Many of these items were broken, dirty, rusted, or just falling apart.

There has been a recent wave of revitalization among buildings in the Shockoe Valley and Tobacco Row Historic District. Where buildings could not be restored, they were demolished, and replaced with new construction. Unfortunately, this particular warehouse did not survive the renewal taking place in this district. Since these photos were taken, the C&O Freight Receiving Depot has been demolished. The site is now used as a gravel parking lot. It is a shame that this building could not be saved. However, the overall architecture of this neighborhood has much improved in recent years. Where a decade prior there were dilapidated brick buildings with an unknown fate, there are now several gleaming residential apartment complexes. This area is now a patchwork of rehabilitated historic buildings and new buildings alike, developing this district into a fine example of how to integrate industrial character with modern city living.

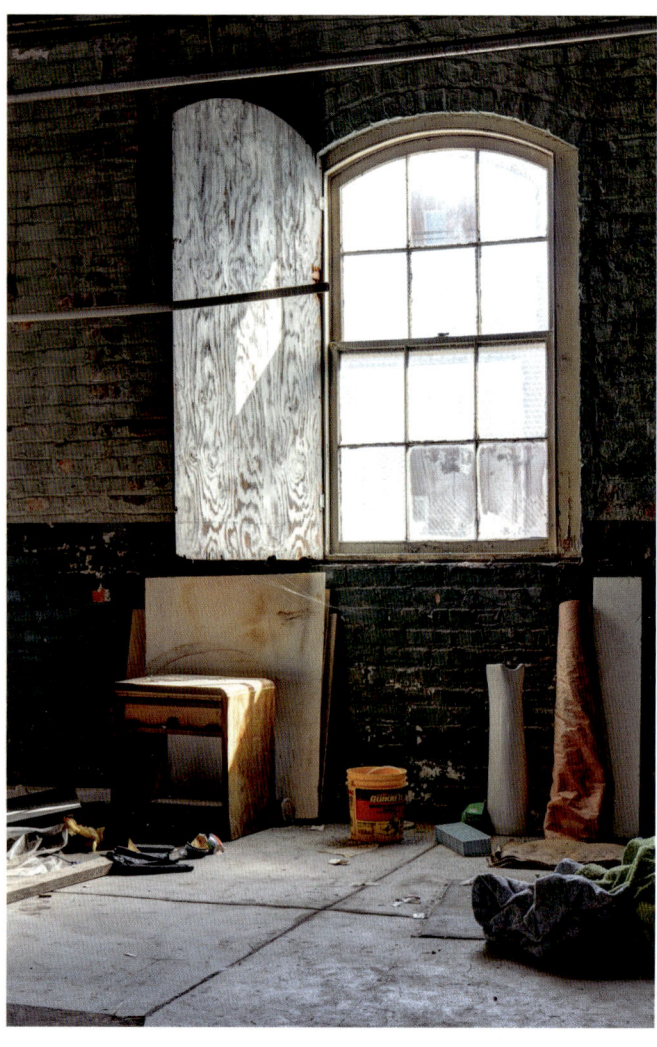

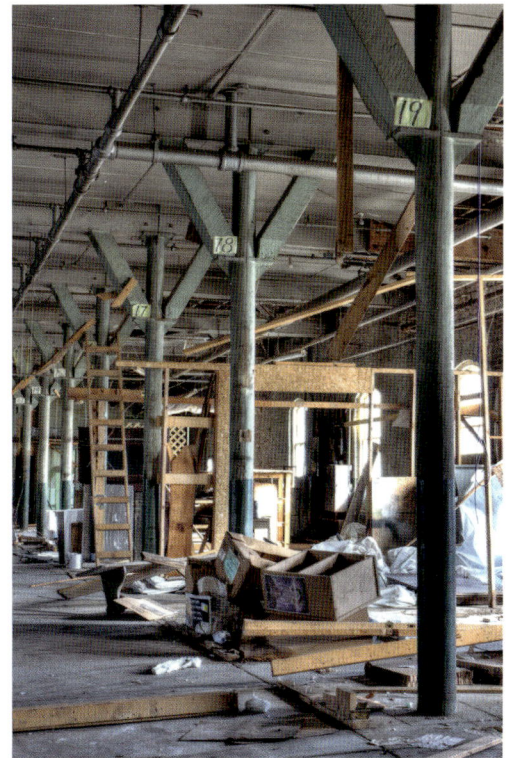

Right: The vertical columns inside this warehouse were made of wood, which would have been more common in the early 1900s than it is today.

Below right: Among other things, this warehouse contained the remains of a piano.

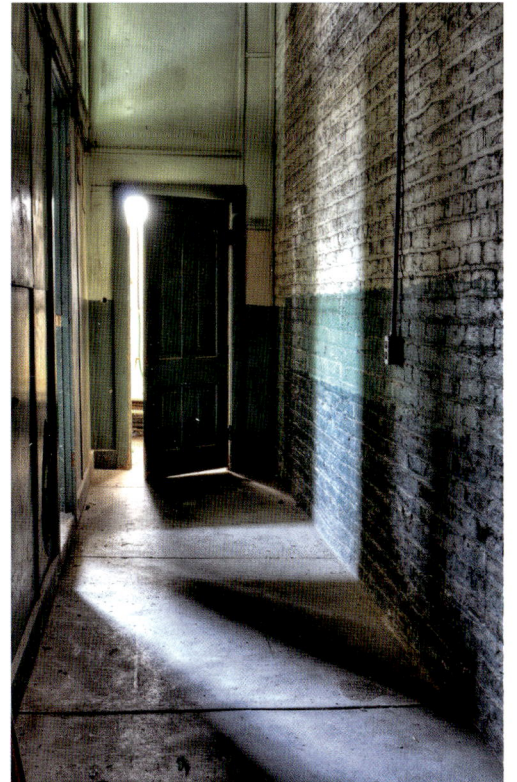

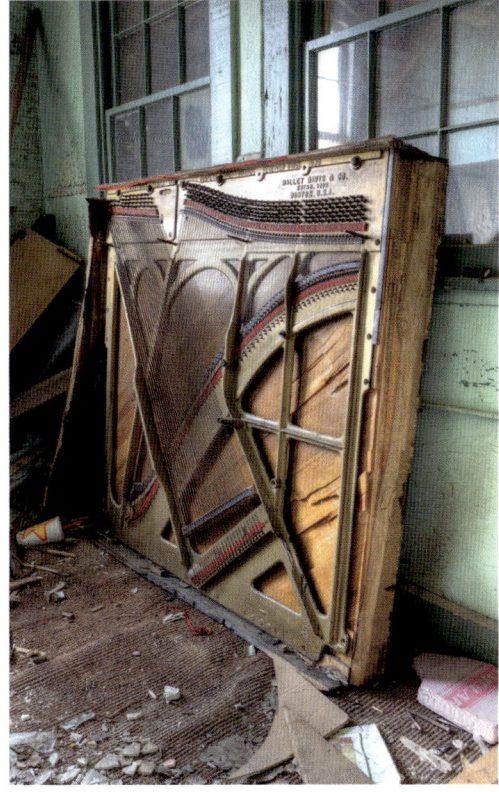

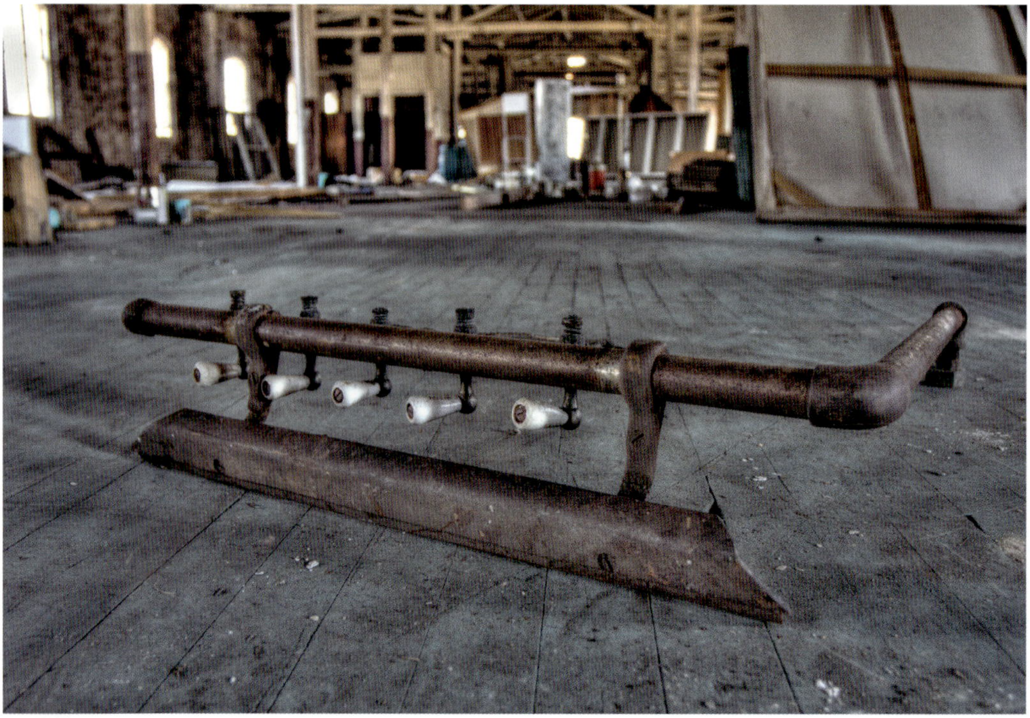

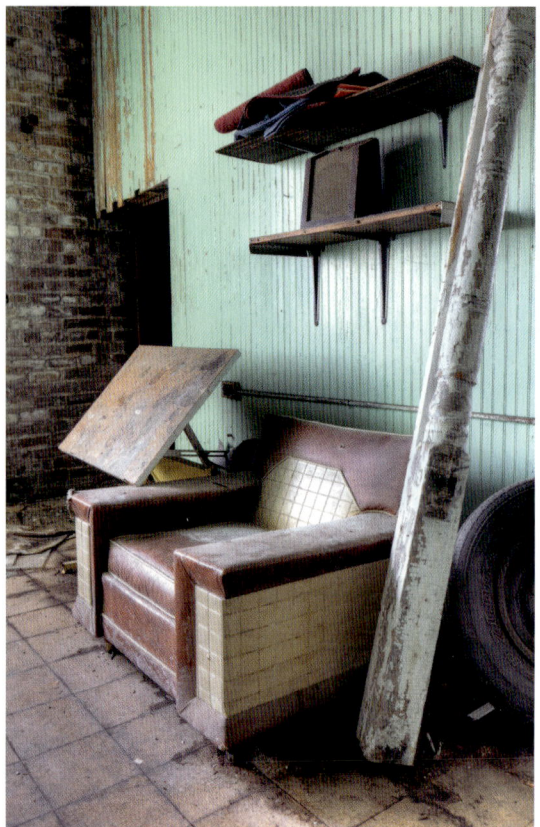

Above: A section of pipe with a series of valves.

Left: An unusual chair sits under a layer of dirt and grime.

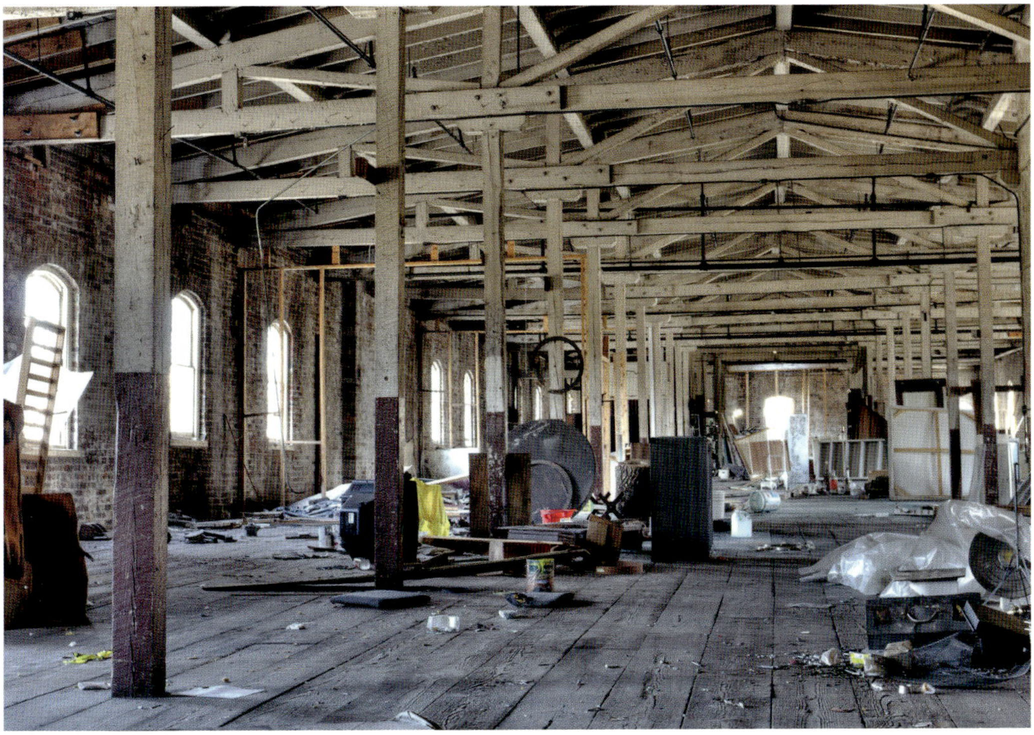

The upper floor was more sparsely cluttered than the lower floor.

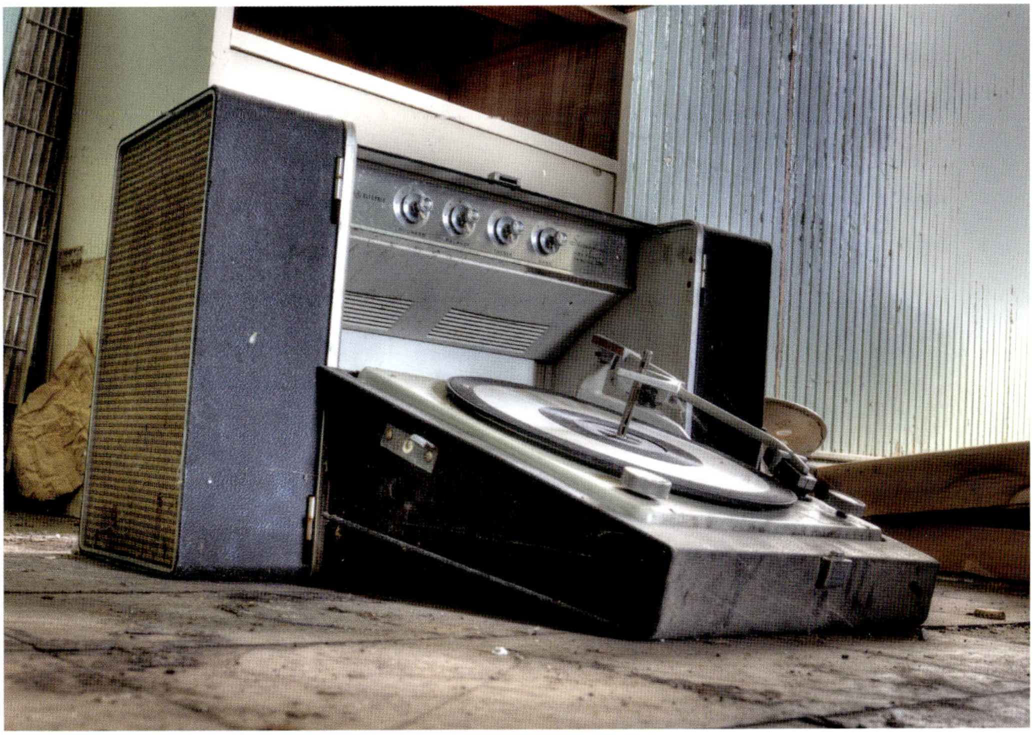

This portable record player from General Electric looks to be from the 1960s.

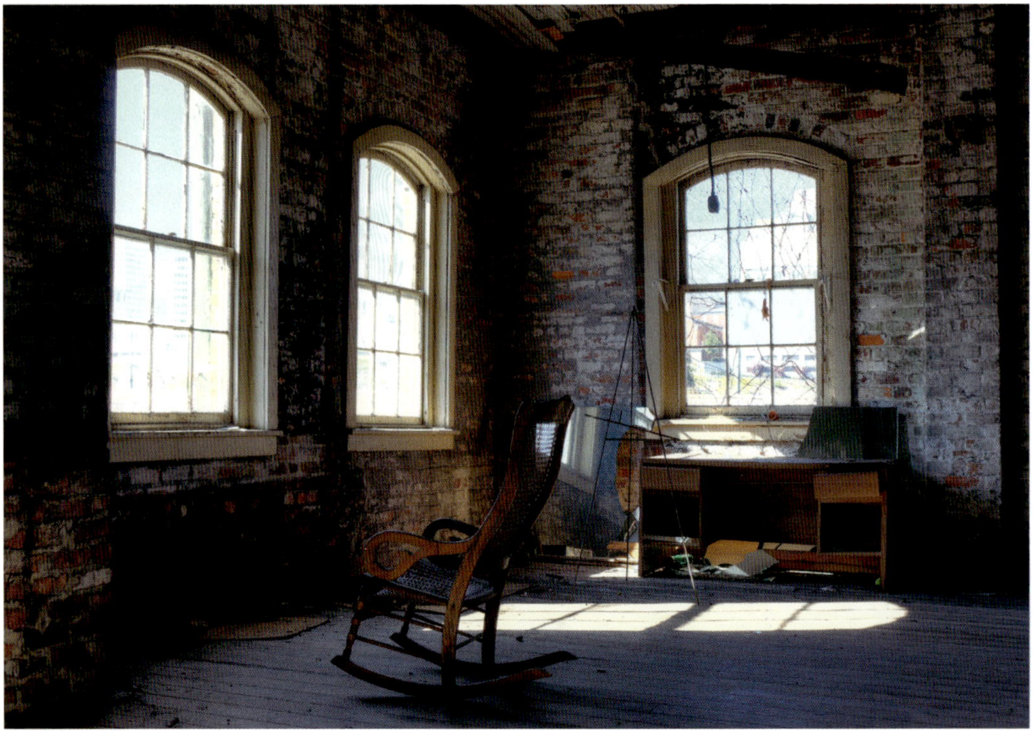

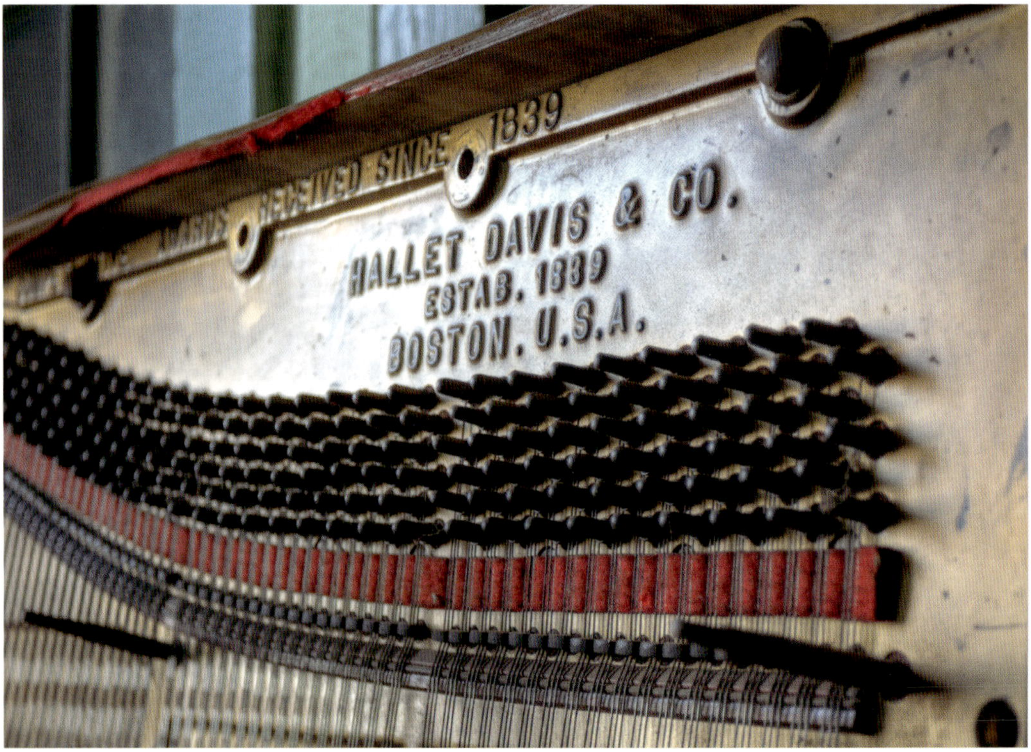

A close-up shot of the unclaimed piano.

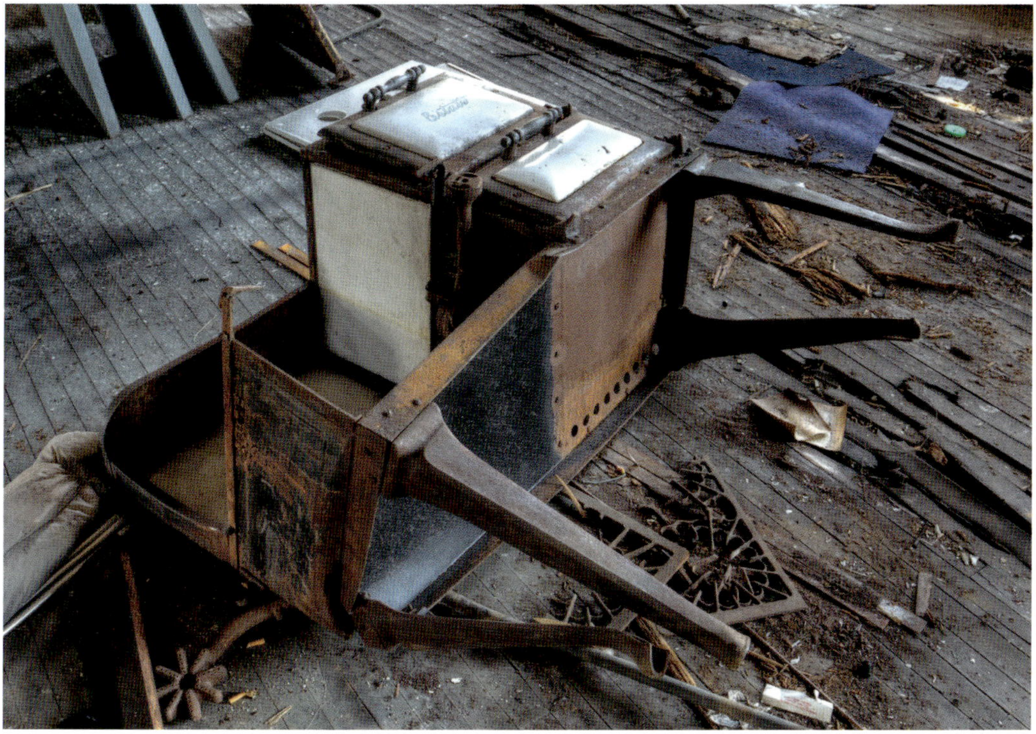

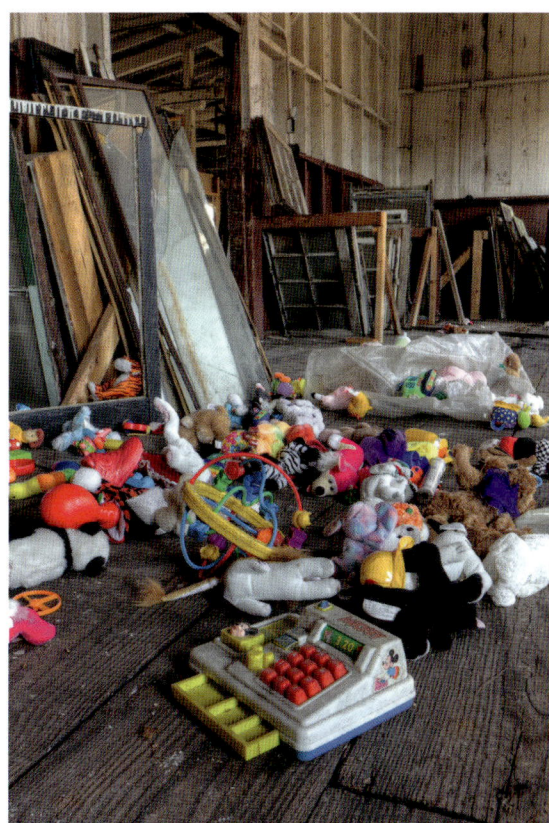

Above: A gas stove from the 1920s, possibly as old as the building itself!

Right: This pile of assorted toys was an unusual find in a dilapidated warehouse.

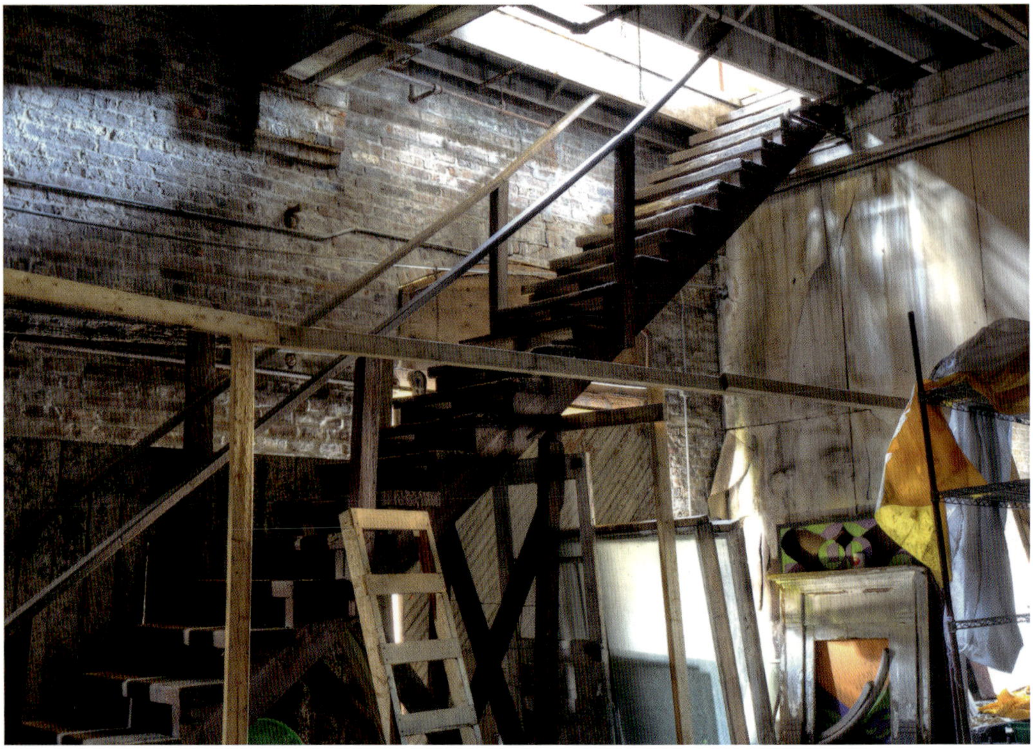

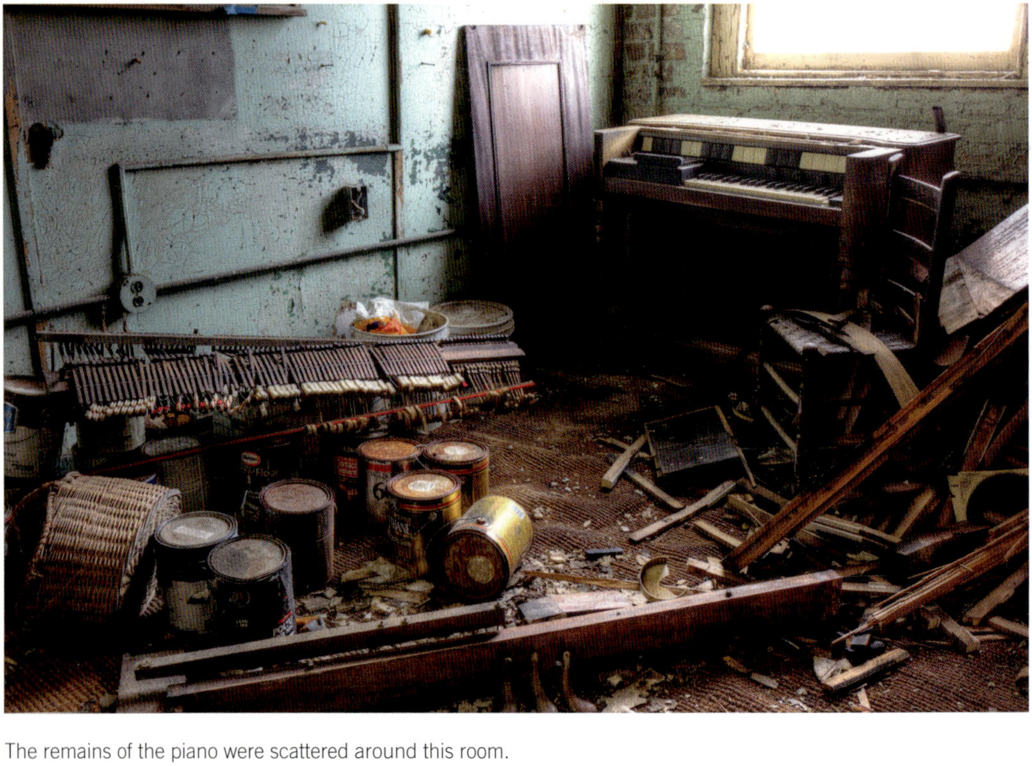

The remains of the piano were scattered around this room.

3

HOUSE IN THE WOODS

AMELIA COURTHOUSE, VA

Tucked away in a small pocket of forest covering only a few acres, there is a house that seems to have been completely forgotten. Since the house cannot be seen from the road, you would never know it is there unless you ventured into the woods.

The structure of this house was in rough condition. Several upstairs walls were sagging, and there were substantial holes in multiple portions of the roof. One pleasant surprise was finding a turkey vulture in one of the upstairs rooms. He did not stick around for long, for upon being discovered, he promptly took flight and exited through a hole in the roof.

Behind the house I found the remains of a rusted 1940 Buick. While all the body panels and wheels appeared intact, the interior was reduced to a collection of wire seat frames. While not a perfectly scientific approach, the age of an abandoned vehicle can sometimes give a clue regarding how much time has passed since a house was vacated. This house had likely been abandoned for several decades. As far as I know, it is still there, hiding in its own little personal thicket.

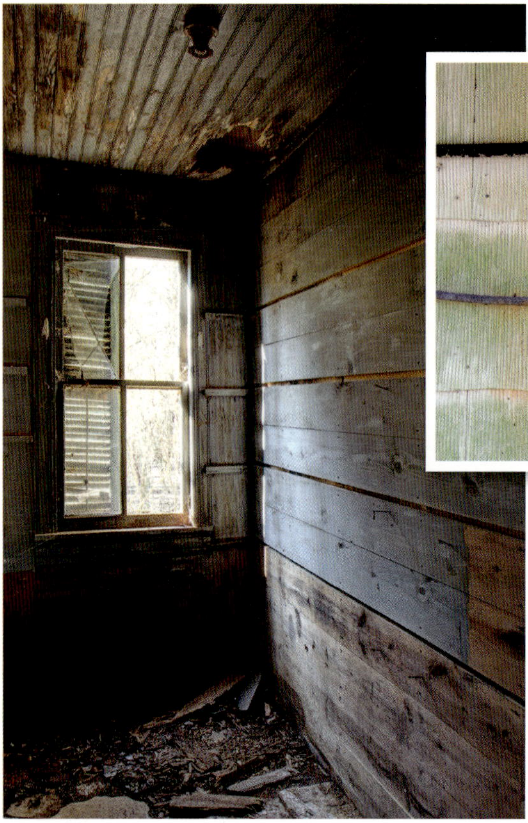

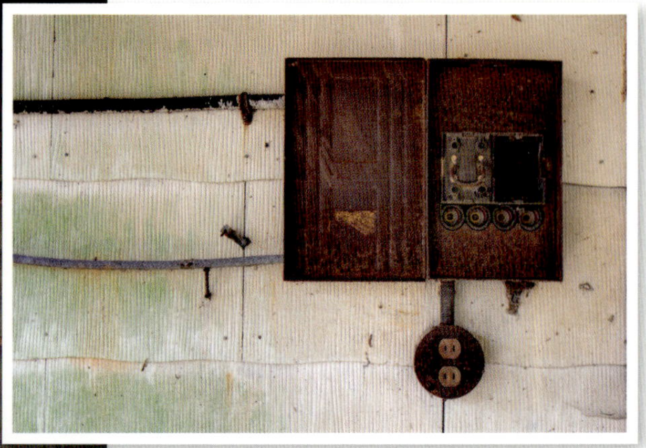

Left: This window is in a small side room on the ground floor.

Below: Deteriorating walls have left behind surprisingly bright colors.

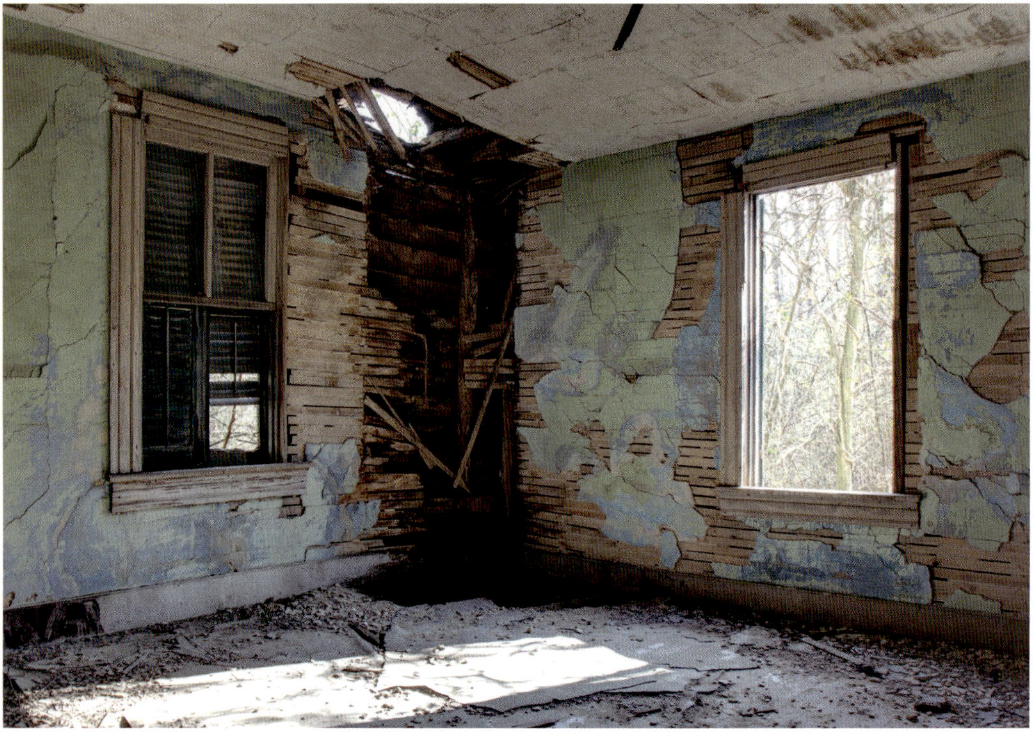

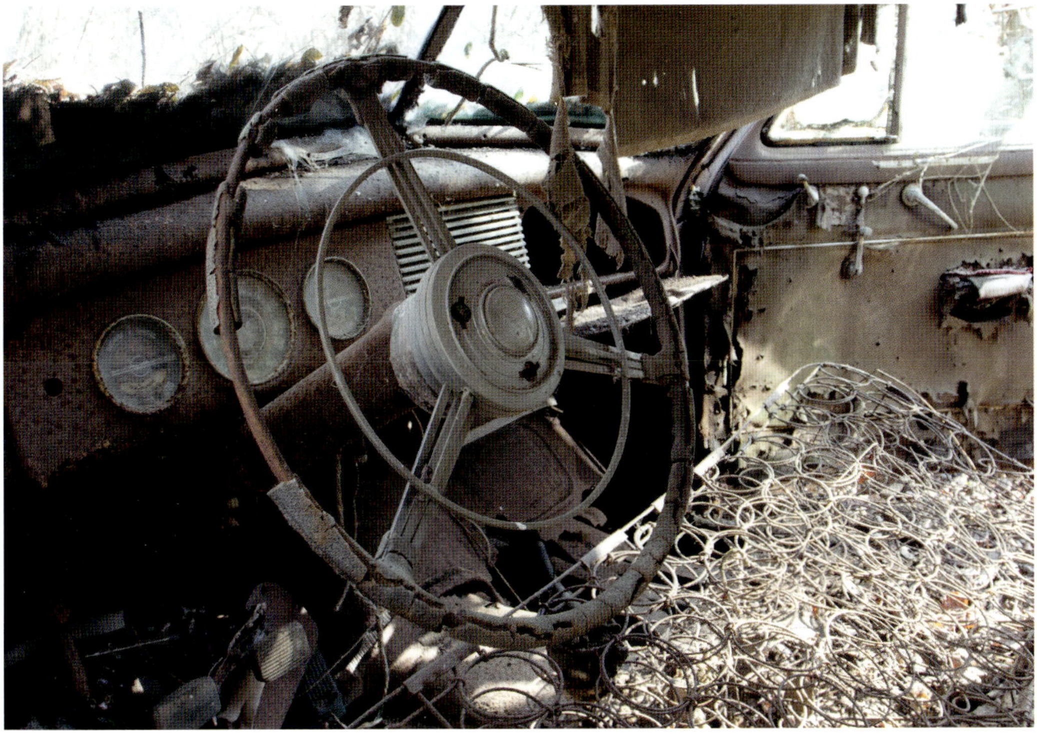

Rust has overwhelmed the interior of this 1940 Buick in the forest.

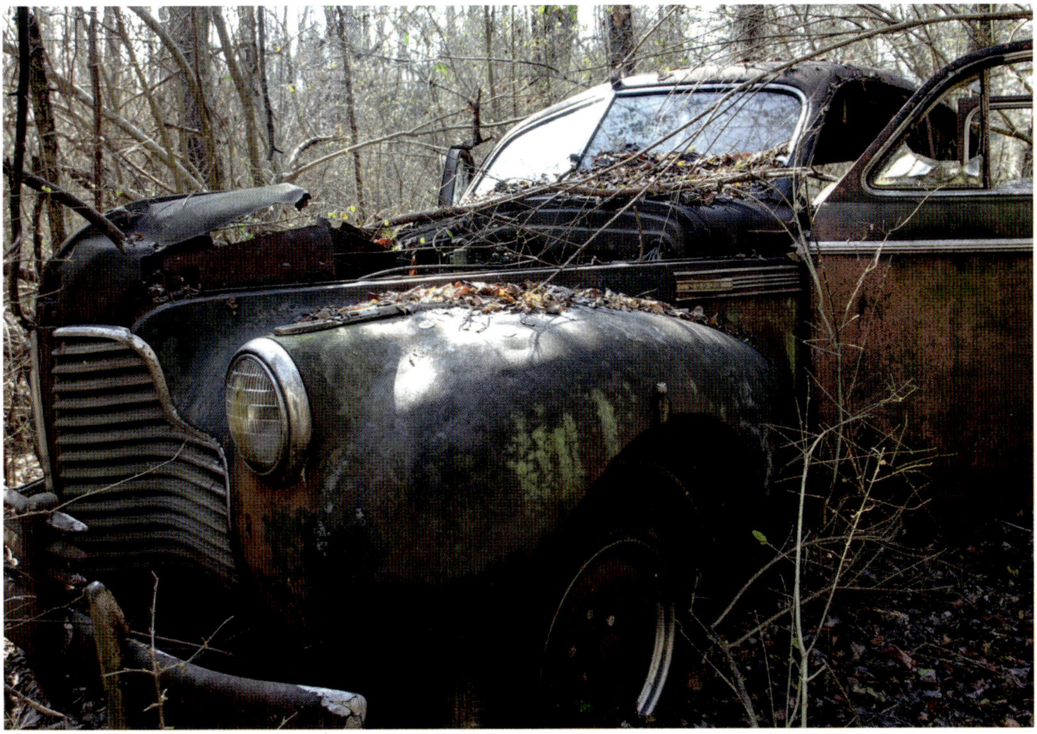

This car has been sitting here in the woods for several decades.

4

FEDERATED PAPER BOARD COMPANY MILL

RICHMOND, VA

One of the driving forces behind the development of Richmond was the diverse industrial presence in the city. This paper mill, the Federated Paper Board Company, was situated in the Manchester Warehouse Historic District. It was part of a small pocket of industrial buildings constructed just south of the James River, in an area referred to as "the falls."

Other industries previously operating in this area included textile mills, iron foundries, flour mills, and tobacco warehouses. Formerly known as the independent City of Manchester, this city thrived as both a railroad destination and as a major port on the James River. The buildings in this area represented a variety of architectural styles, and reflect high-quality masonry construction from the turn of the twentieth century. The City of Manchester was annexed by the City of Richmond in 1910, and many residents now refer to this area as "Old Town Manchester" or "Historic Manchester." Commercial activity in Manchester declined steadily during the second half of the twentieth century. However, the district has experienced a recent revival of sorts, as many of the former industrial buildings have been converted into residential apartments.[1]

Power for the mill operations at Federated Paper Board Company was originally provided by the adjacent Manchester Canal and James River. When the Richmond Flood Wall was constructed in 1995, it separated the mill buildings from the James River.[2]

One beautiful feature visible from inside this building was the manner in which sunlight scattered through the windows, many of which had been painted over and partially obscured. This resulted in pinpoints of sunlight scattering across the floor, though the overall interior remained low-lit and shadowed. The wood flooring in this building was disintegrating rapidly, but the masonry structure seemed relatively stable. The underground level seemed almost like a catacombs, with concrete columns and sunlight filtering down from above.

There have been many names applied to this paper mill over the course of a century. It has existed as the Federated Paper Board Company, the Manchester Board and Paper Company, and also as the Standard Paper Company. The building was most recently owned by Caraustar Industries. The last commercial use of the building was in 2008. As a result of chemical leeching and industrial pollution in the building, the structure was deemed unsuitable for human occupation, and the remains of the paper mill were demolished in 2019.[3]

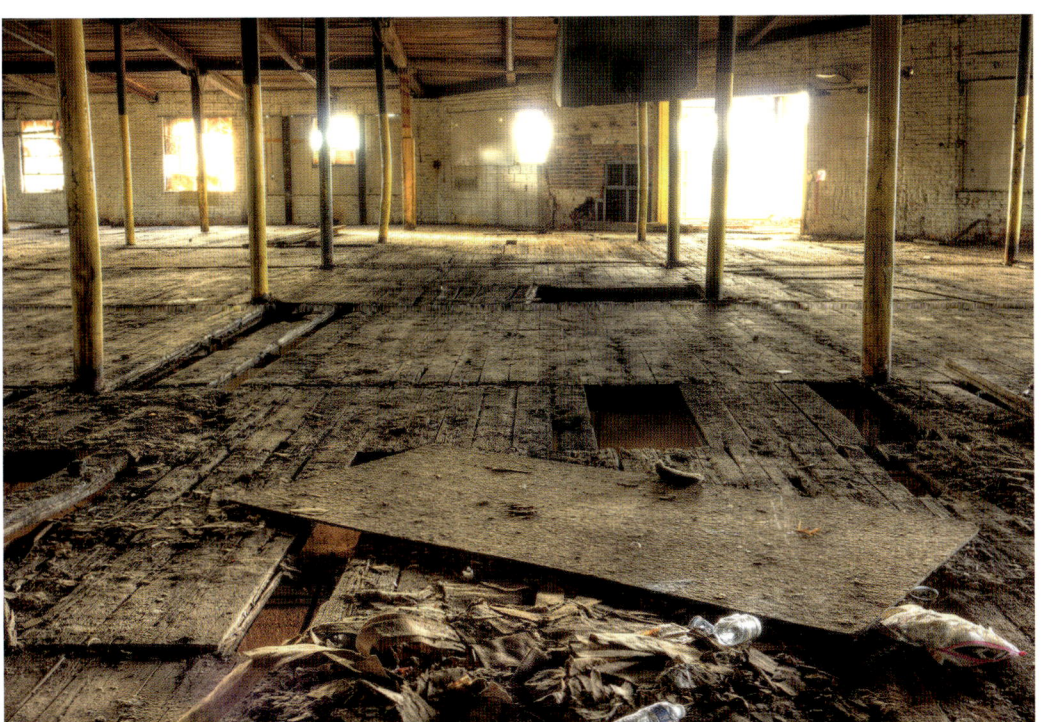

Not much remains of the upper floor, just the deteriorating floor and yellow poles.

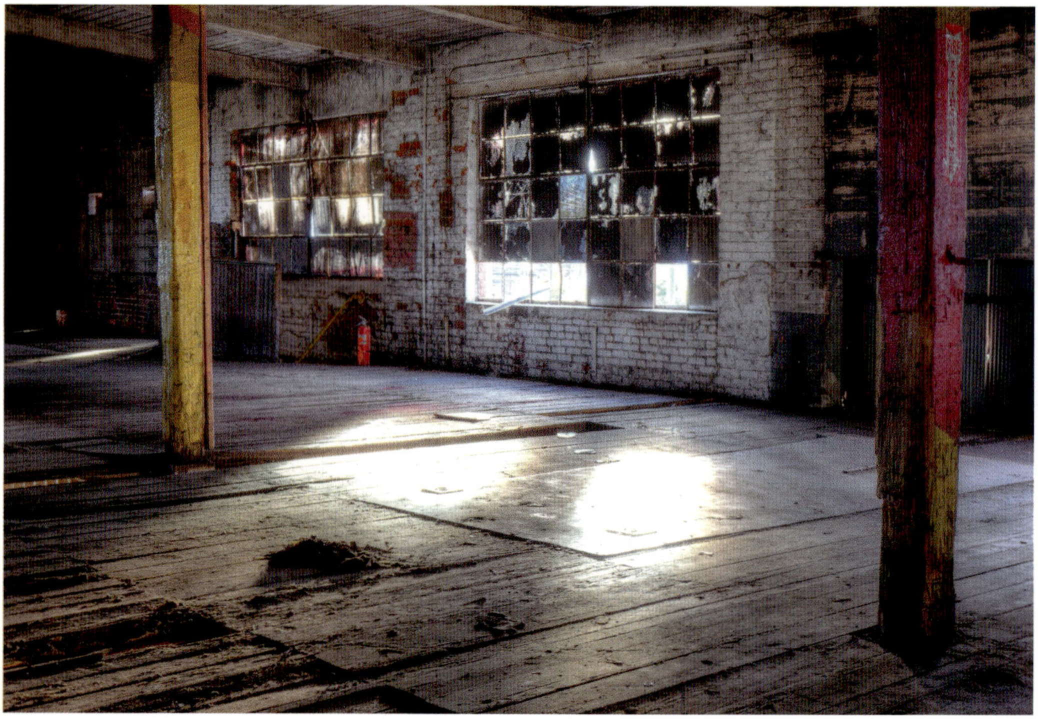

Light streams through a combination of tinted windows and broken windowpanes.

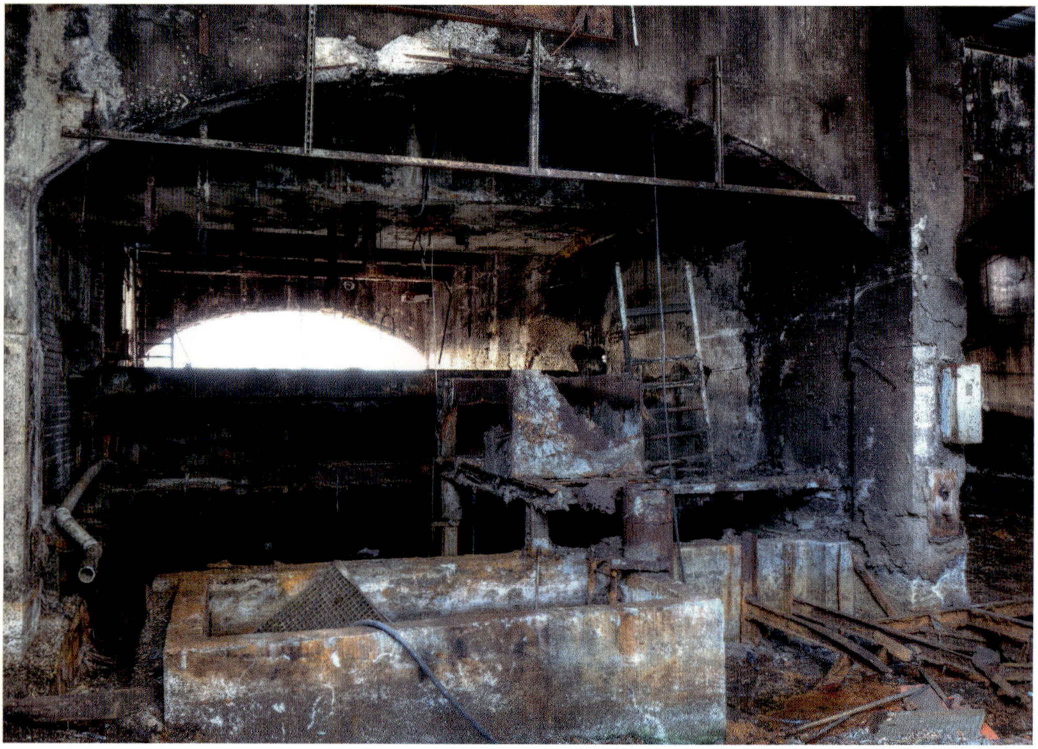

The underground section had the feel of a catacombs.

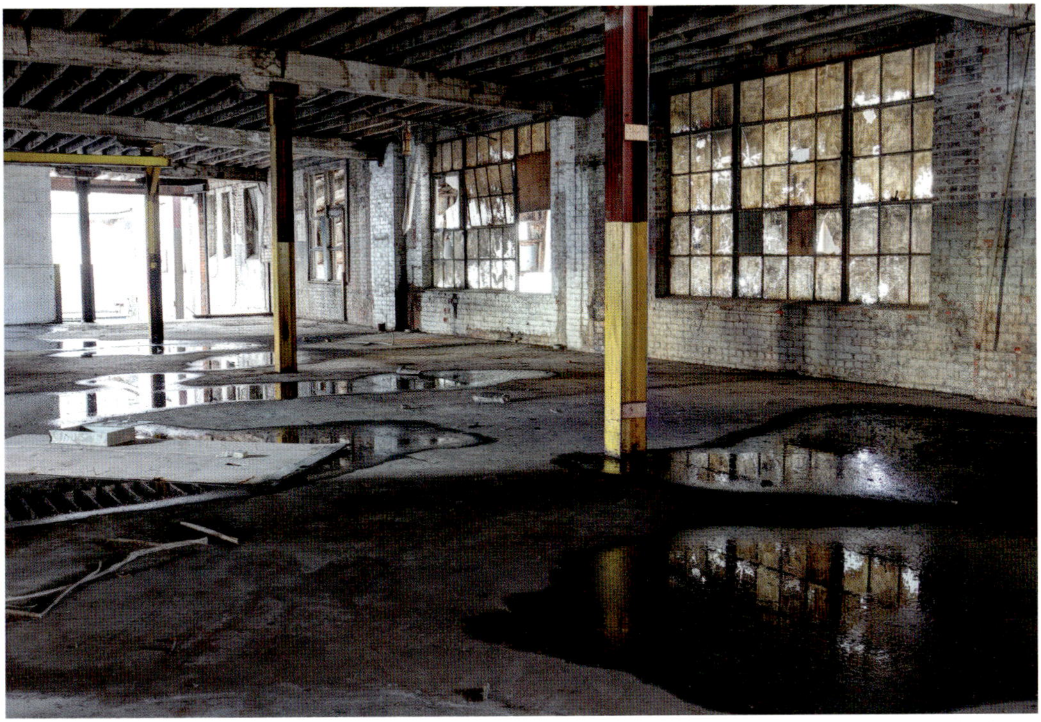

Standing water offered a nice set of reflections.

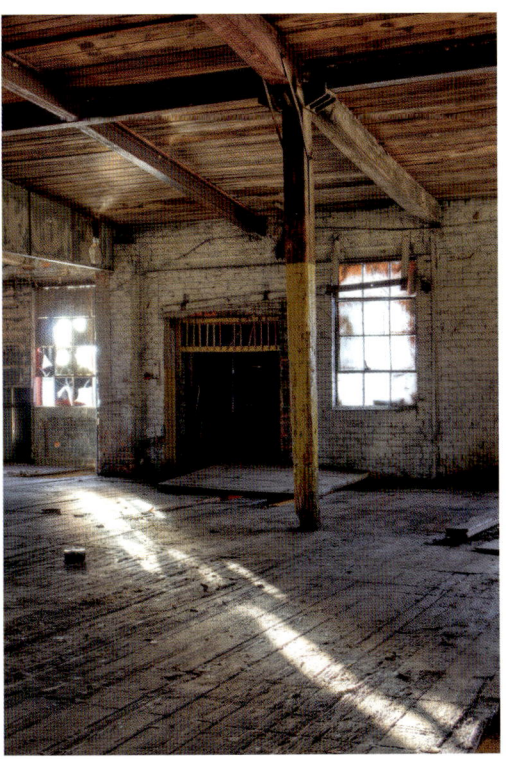

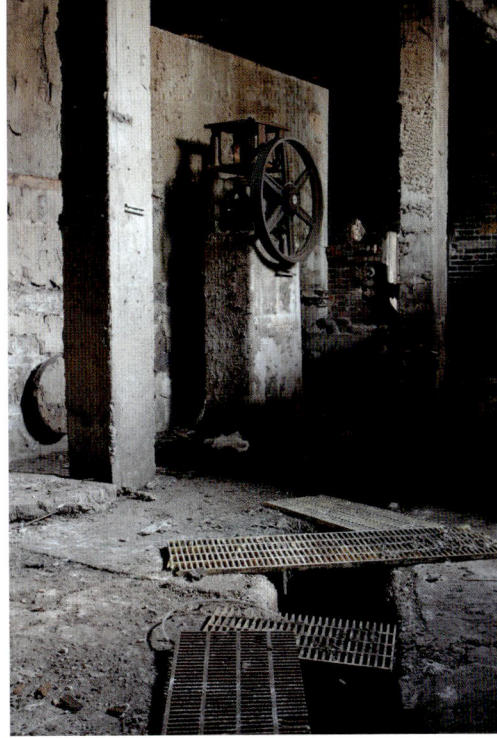

Above right: This section of the underground level requires you to watch where you step.

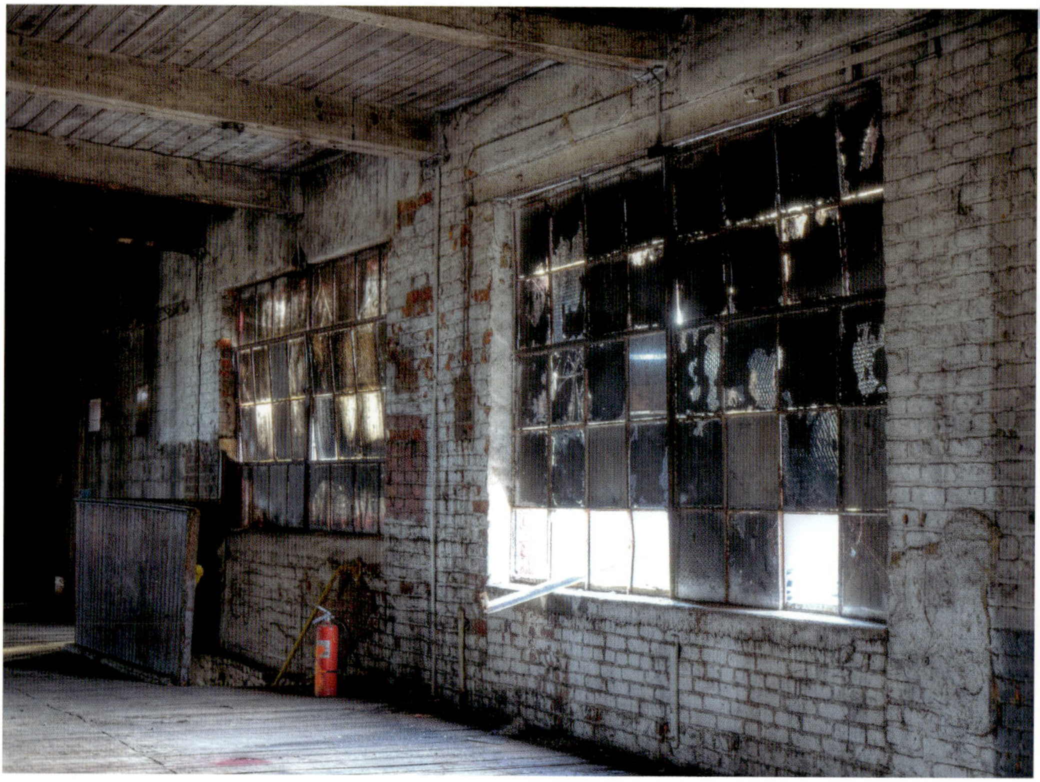

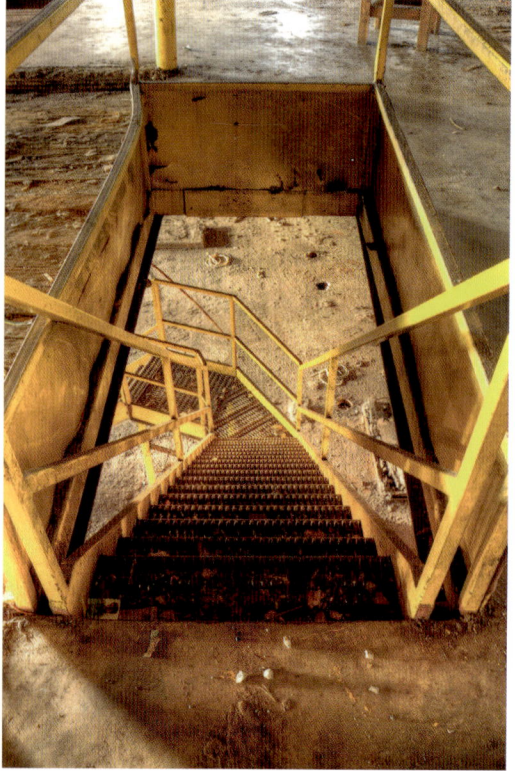

This staircase placed in the middle of the floor was painted yellow for good reason.

5

VIRGINIA RENAISSANCE FAIRE

FREDERICKSBURG, VA

Without a doubt, the Virginia Renaissance Faire is the most unique abandoned property that I have ever explored. This Tudor-style campus consists primarily of stone and wood structures, designed to imitate a medieval style of architecture. The property is situated just off Kings Highway in Fredericksburg, and locals refer to this area as Sherwood Forest, which seems the perfect place for some Renaissance-era cosplay.[1]

Prior to construction, the land for this renaissance faire was purchased by Renaissance Entertainment Corp, a company that operates similar events in cities around the United States. The first year for the Virginia Renaissance Faire was in 1996; however, due to poor weather and declining ticket sales, the faire was closed by 1999.[2] During my time on the property I found the ticketing building at the former park entrance, and it was full of thousands of unsold tickets. You can even see the year 1997 on the ticket roll that I photographed. After closure, this renaissance faire was relocated southwest to Lake Anna Winery and it has been operating there with much more success than the original location.[3]

Walking around this landscape was absolutely surreal. All the buildings were partially obscured by years of undergrowth. There were no remnants of any paths or walkways. These unusual houses just seemed to be scattered randomly in an overgrown field. It almost seemed like I was walking through a small medieval village that was just vacated by its residents, and then forgotten. There was also very little in the way of vandalism. Besides some broken trim on doorways and windows, the structures were essentially intact. As I explored these buildings and examined their details, I was constantly reminded of how much effort went into creating an event that only occurred a few months out of the year. It is estimated that the total cost to purchase this land and construction the renaissance faire exceeded $5 million.[4]

Moored on the edge of a small pond, located in the center of the renaissance faire, was a small-scale medieval sailing ship. This is definitely the crown jewel of the entire landscape. The pond must have partially dried up over the years, because the ship now rests on a patch of dry land. The undersized ship was used for theatrical performances, but now it just stands as a reminder of the sheer creativity and zeal that went into building this place.

The future of this property remains uncertain. After the closure of the renaissance faire, the property was sold in 2001, and it is currently used by a local sportsman and hunting club.[5] The marshy quality of the land makes development opportunities questionable, but there has been some interest in converting the properties for industrial uses.[6] It would be a valuable act of preservation if these buildings could be refreshed and maintained, and possibly even converted into an attraction for future visitors.

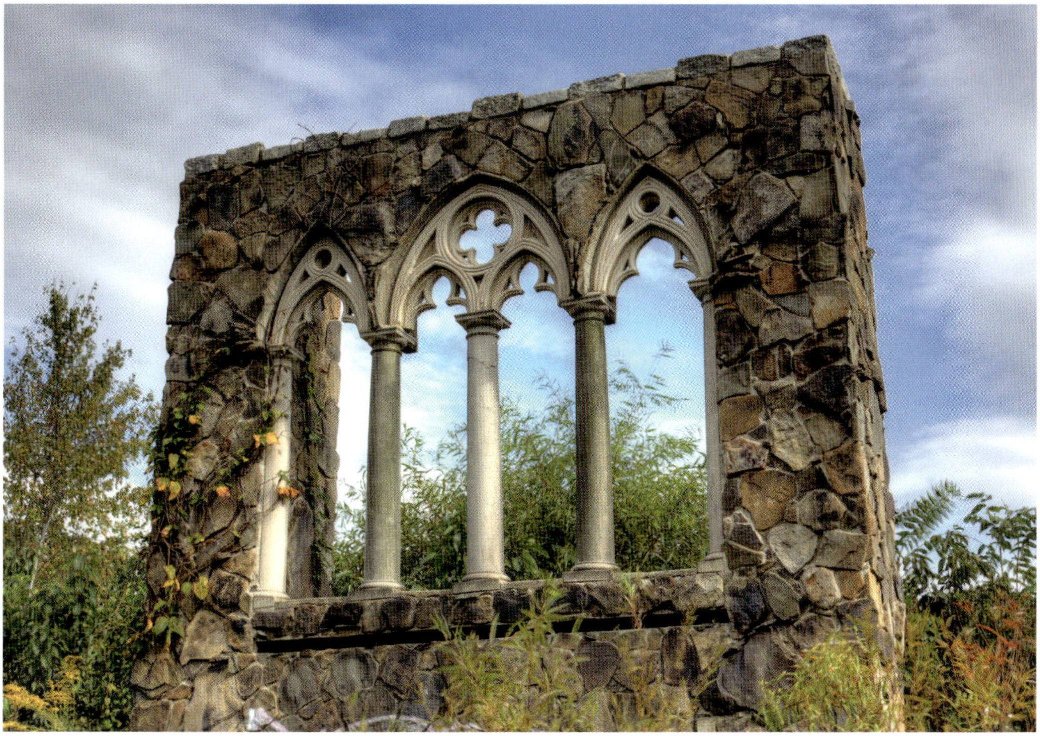

This stone decoration formerly greeted attendees as they entered the property.

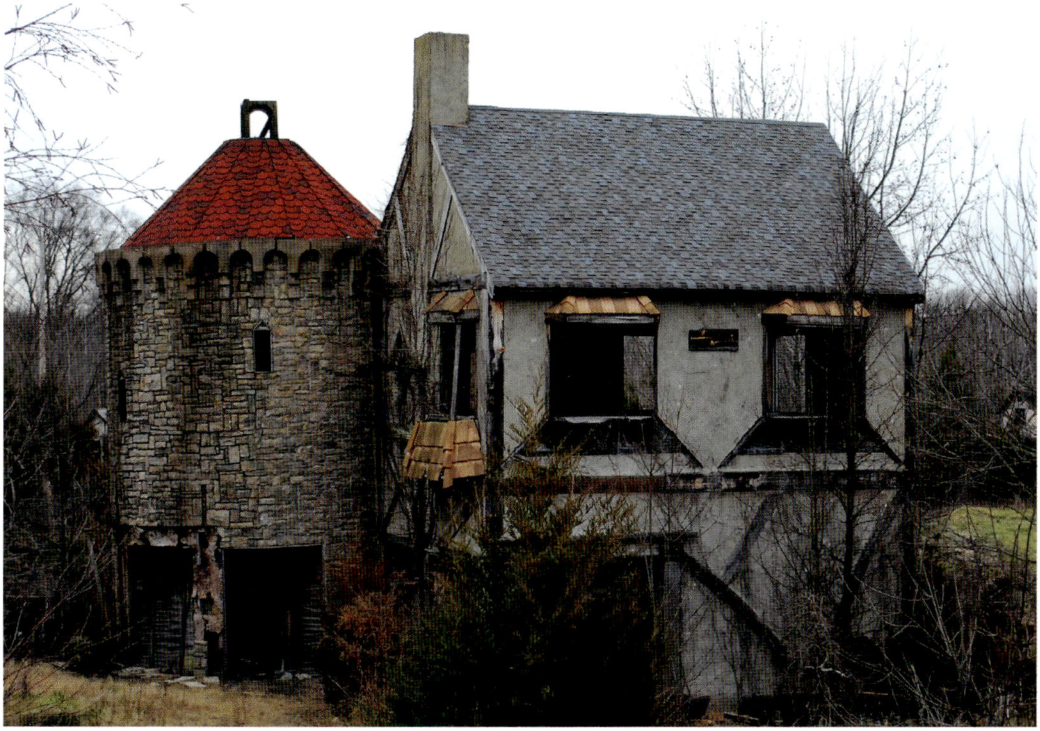

This pair of buildings are among the tallest in the complex.

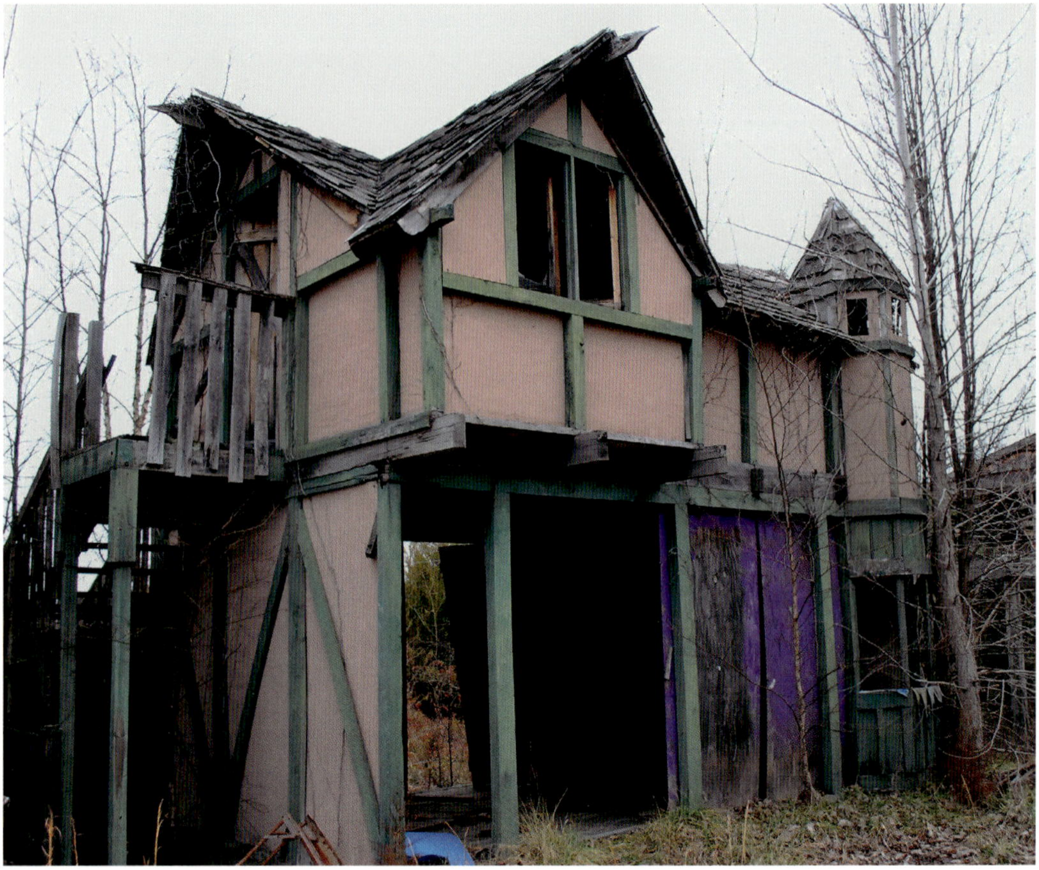

Two decades has taken a toll on the wooden parts of these structures.

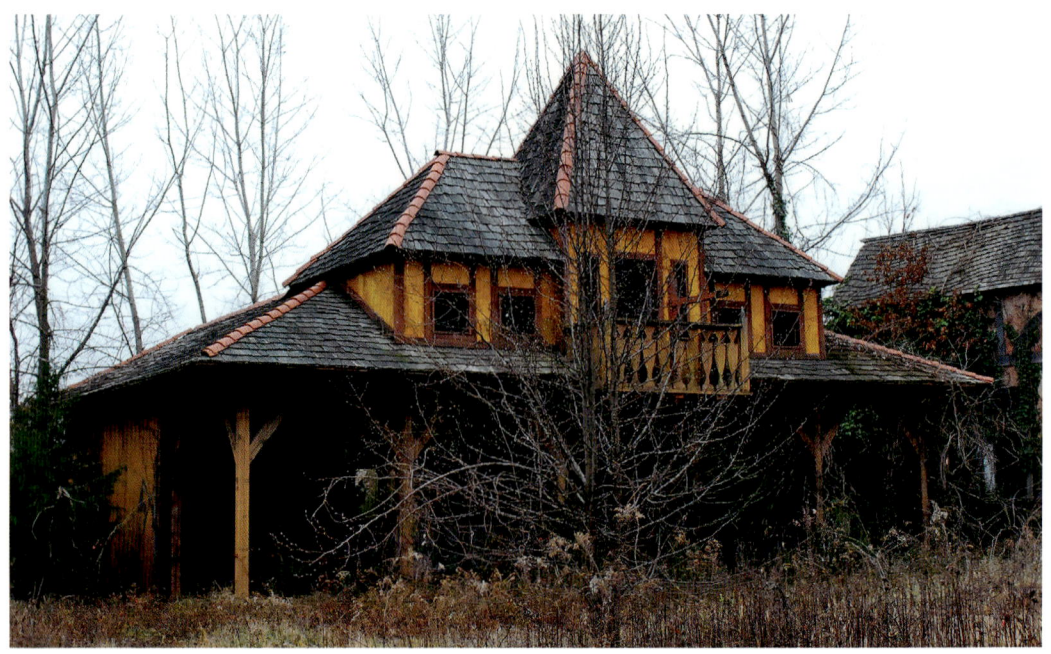

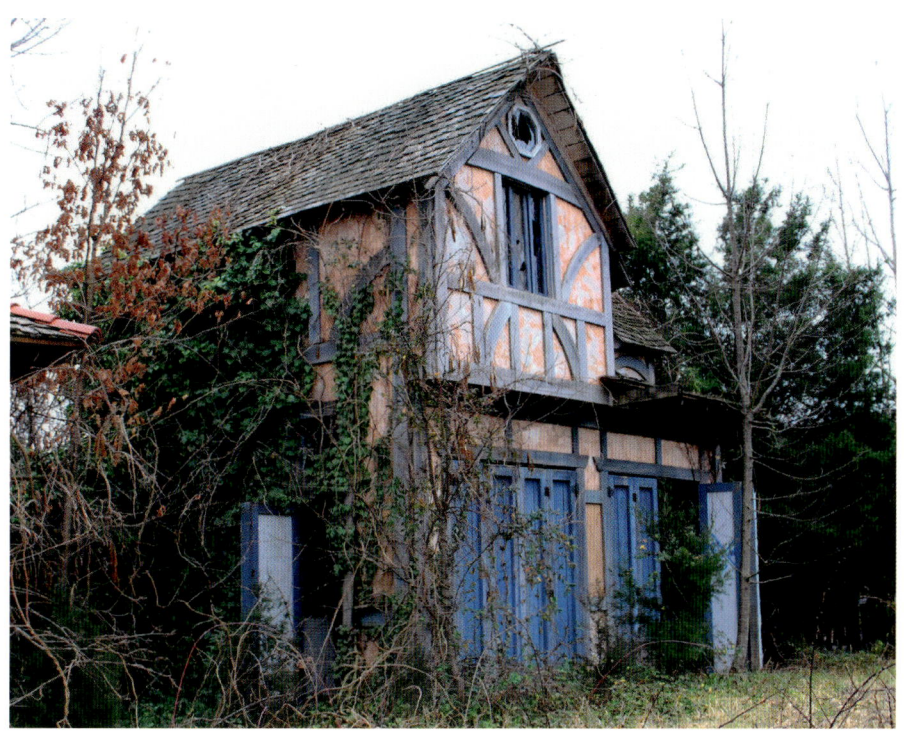

It's impossible to know the purpose of most of these buildings, but they do represent a wide array of designs.

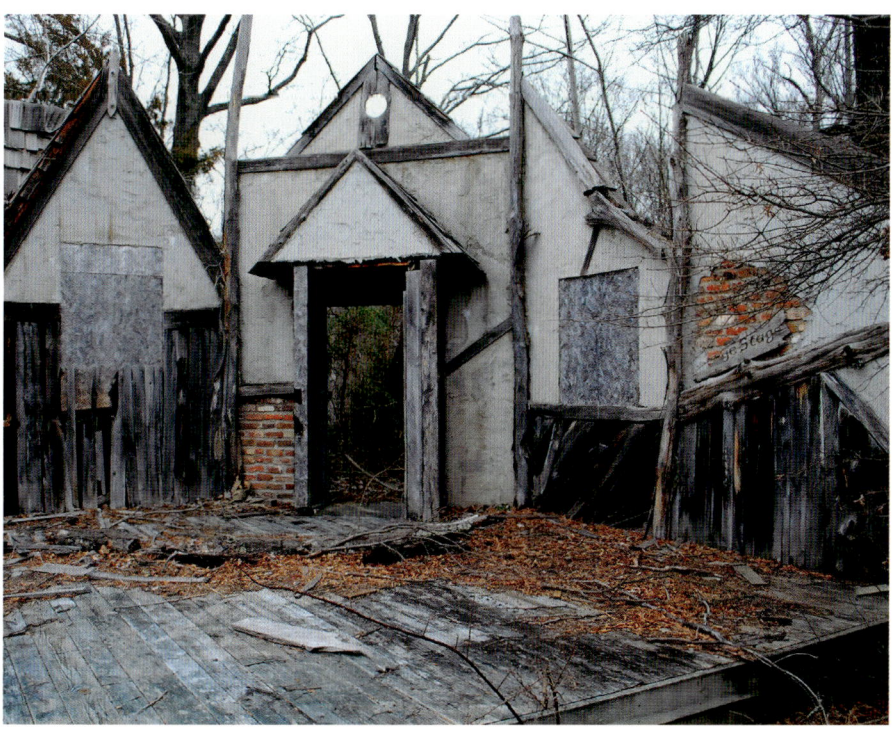

You can imagine the fun performances that once took place on this stage!

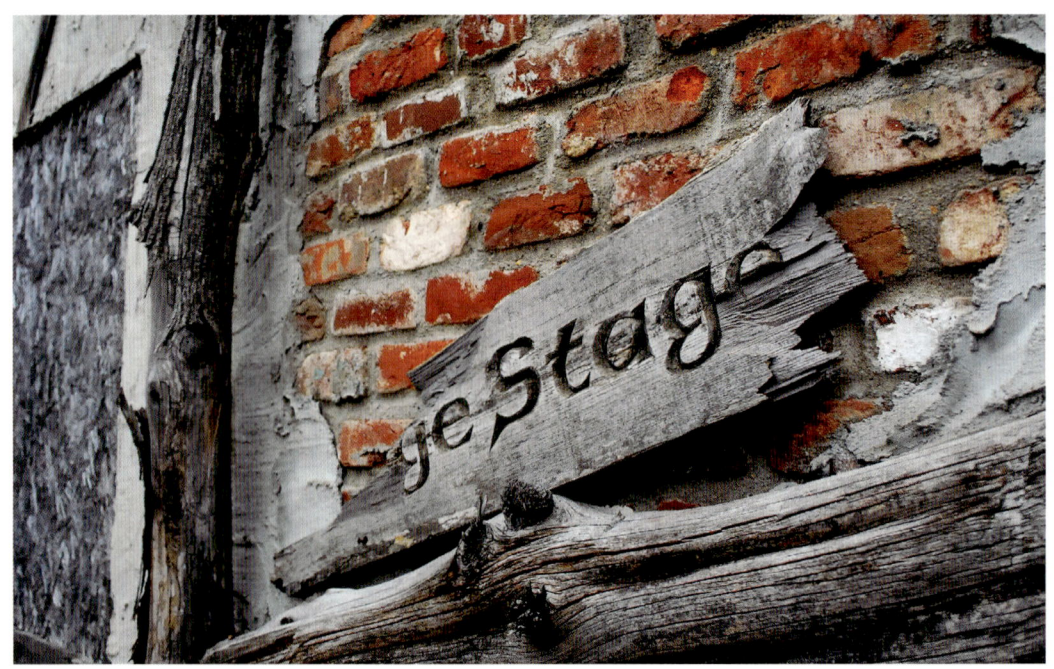

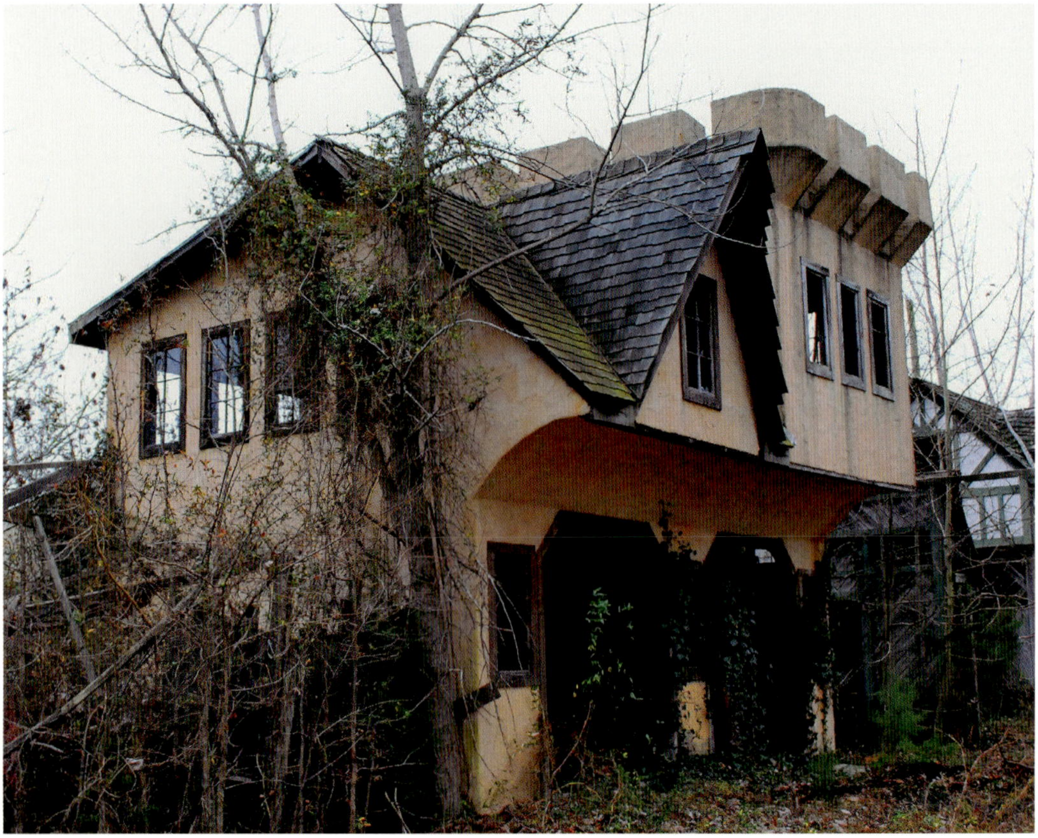

This structure looks like a small castle with a two-car garage.

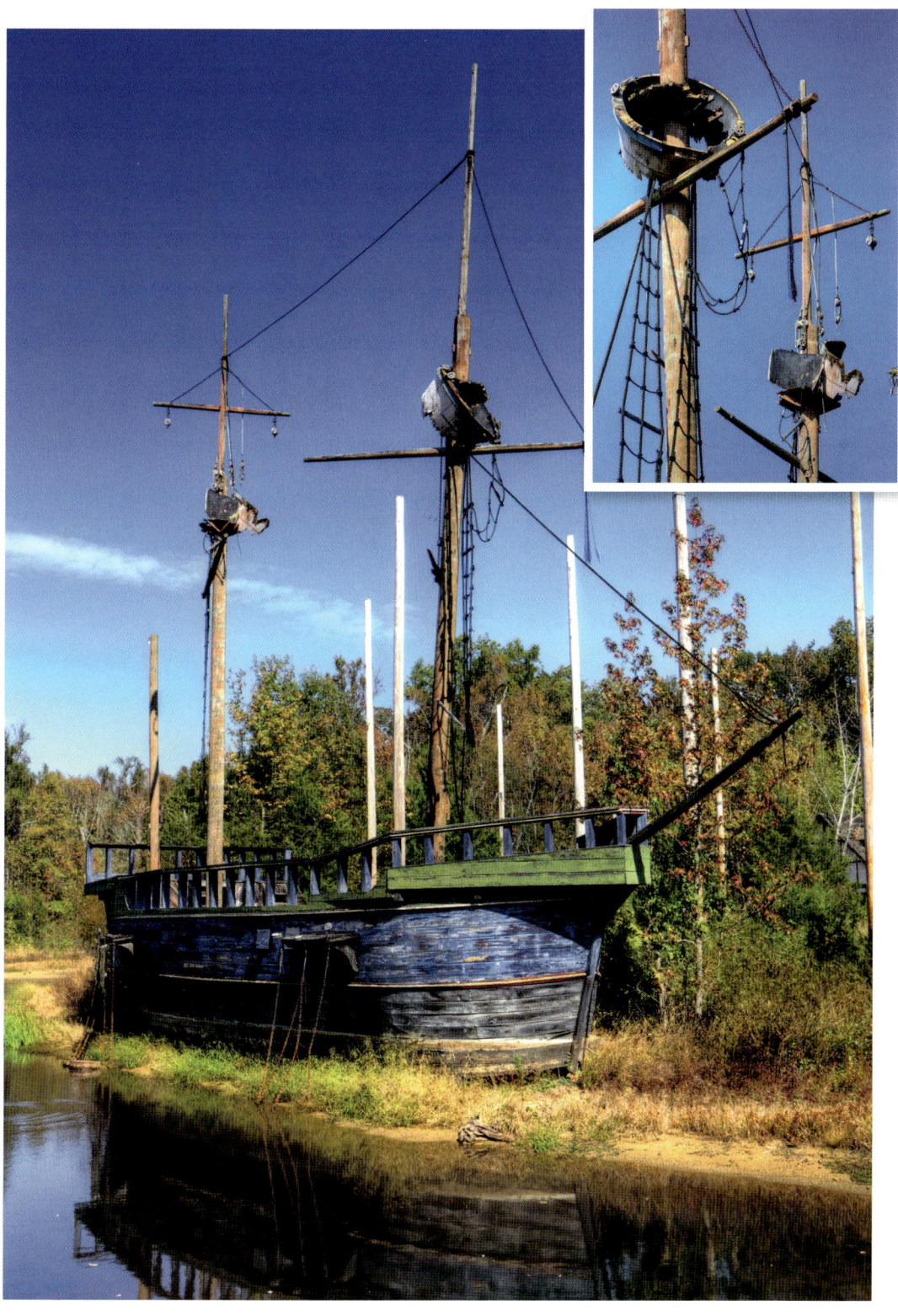

The small-scale medieval ship is still there, but now it is parked on dry land. *Inset:* These crow's nests were probably used for performances of some kind.

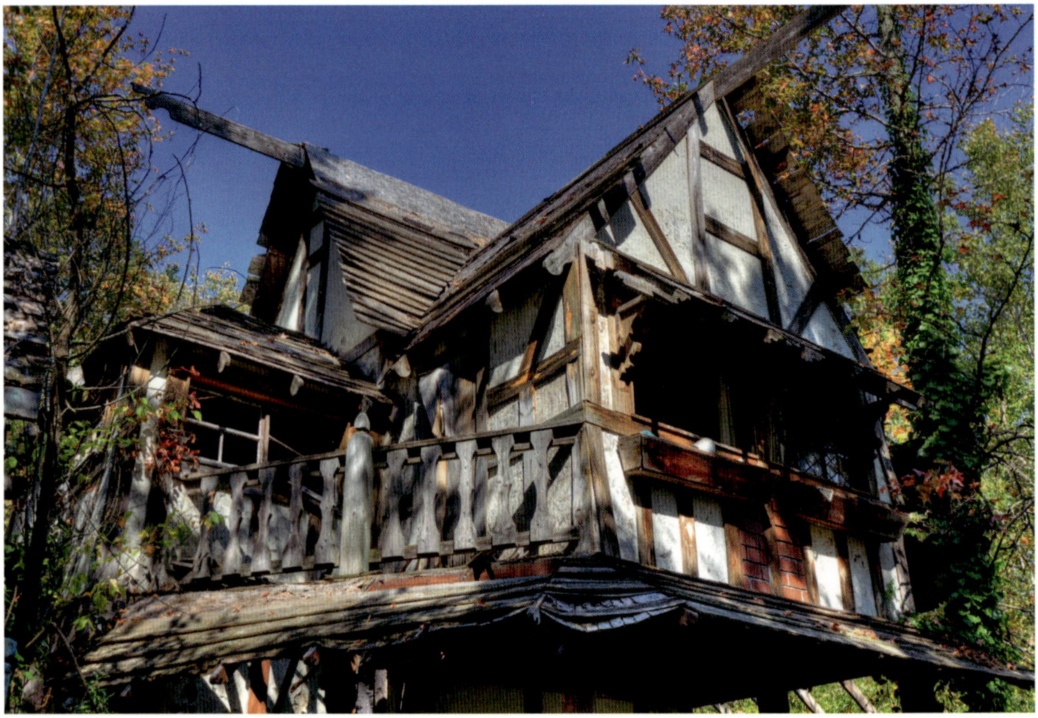

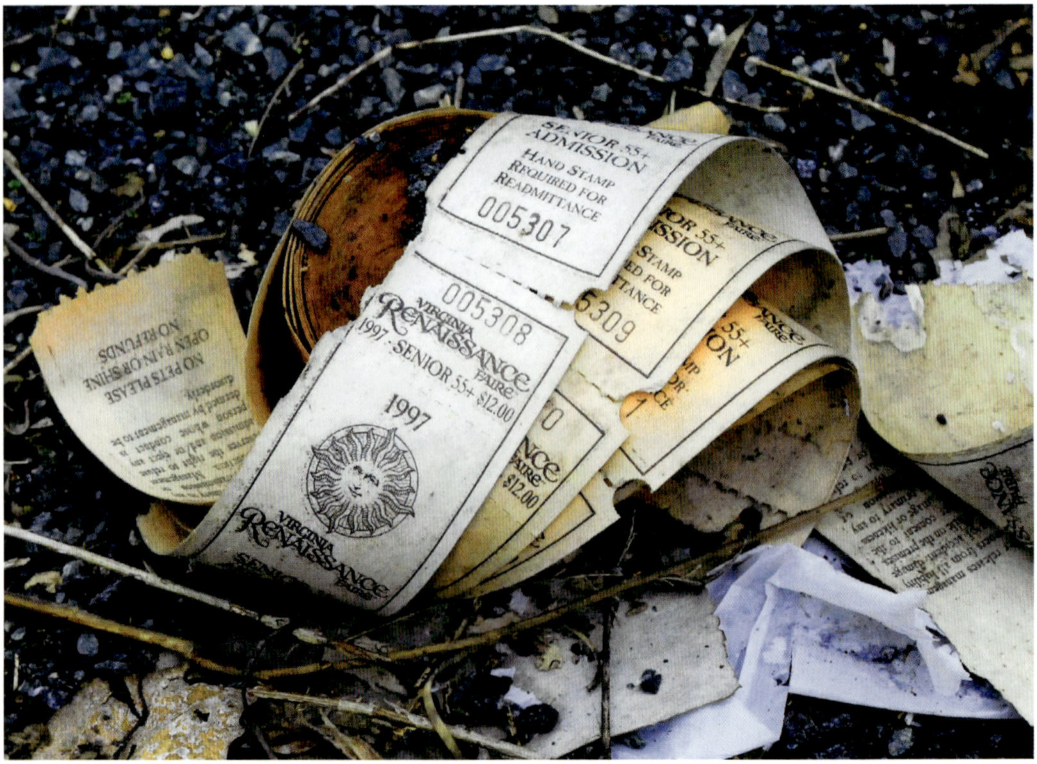

The ground was littered with unused tickets with the year printed on them.

6

SOUTHERN BISCUIT COMPANY

RICHMOND, VA

Known to many local residents as simply "the cookie factory," the Southern Biscuit Company building is a prominent fixture on West Broad Street in Richmond. This six-story industrial building features a small water tower on the roof, along with an elaborate lighted metal sign which reads, "HOME OF FFV COOKIES AND CRACKERS." North of the building rests the former Richmond Fredericksburg and Potomac railway, and the historic Broad Street Station is just to the east.

Construction of this reinforced concrete building began in 1927.[1] The layout of each interior floor included large concrete columns arranged in grids. Each floor also contained steel-framed industrial windows. These windows appeared to have a simple grayish color when viewed from outside the building. But once inside the building, I discovered that there are a variety of color palettes in the window glass. Some panels were mixtures of orange and green, while others were solid yellow. There was also an entire upper floor of windows that were tinted only in shades of blue. When you are inside a commercial building with no artificial lighting, the color of the windows has a tremendous impact on the feel of the building. The colorful windows provided a calming effect that contrasted nicely with the cold emptiness of each floor.

Southern Biscuit Works was founded in Richmond in 1899. The company changed their name to Southern Biscuit Company in 1927, simultaneous with their relocation to this new building. They manufactured cookies, crackers, and cakes that were distributed across the country. This particular factory was the headquarters of Southern Biscuit Company from 1927-2006. They were also the first bakery to commercially produce Girl Scout Cookies, starting in 1939. In the same year, the company also began to sell their products under a new brand name, Famous Foods of Virginia. The company was merged with several other bakeries in 1967, and the new parent company was named Interbake Foods, Inc.[2]

One of the unique features in the cookie production arrangement was that all raw baking ingredients were initially transported to the top floor, where the ovens are located. After the dough was formed for each product, it followed the manufacturing process down through the floors using a system of gravity conveyors. This arrangement helped to reduce the operating cost of the manufacturing process. These ovens were reportedly capable of making up to 640,000 cookies in a single hour.[3] Metal racks inside the oven assembly would hold large trays of products as they baked, and the rotating process was designed to promote even baking.[4] One of the most stunning things about exploring this building was that the ovens still smelled like cookies, even several years after the factory was last in operation.

Commercial use of the building ceased in 2006, when Interbake Foods relocated their production to a new facility in Front Royal, Virginia.[5] I was lucky to see the inside of this building when I did, because after these photos were taken, the building was renovated into residential apartments. The building reopened as Cookie Factory Lofts in 2014. Common areas of the building have been decorated with factory photos taken during the building's time as a cookie bakery. Developers also took the time to refurbish the rooftop metal sign, and it illuminates the Richmond skyline once again.

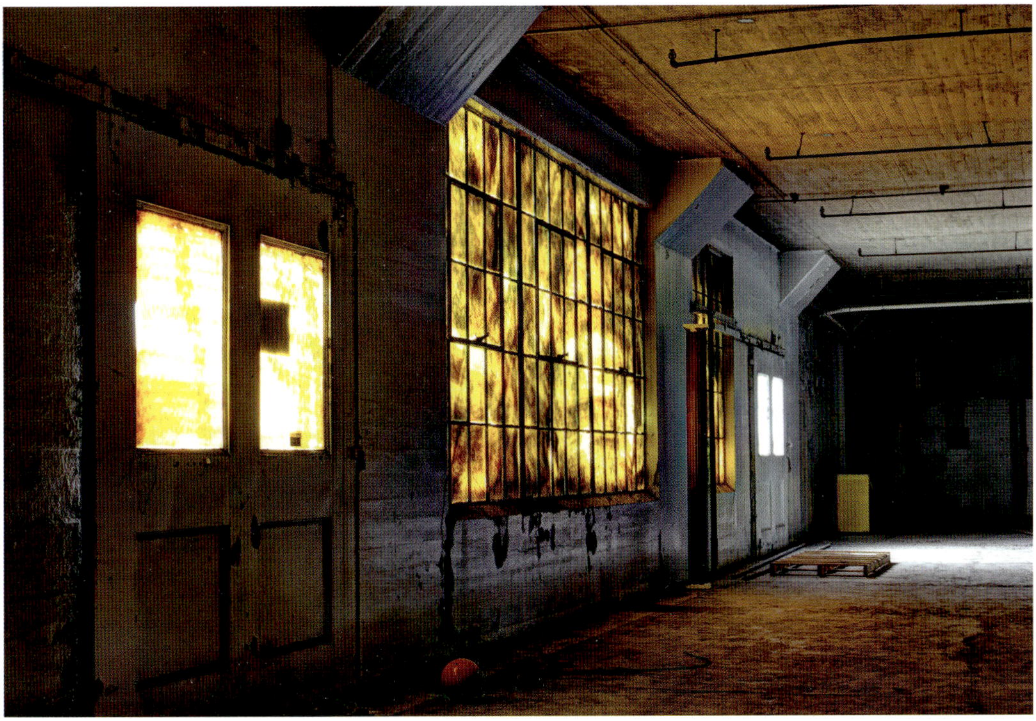

Yellow-tinted windows cast a warm glowing light onto the interior.

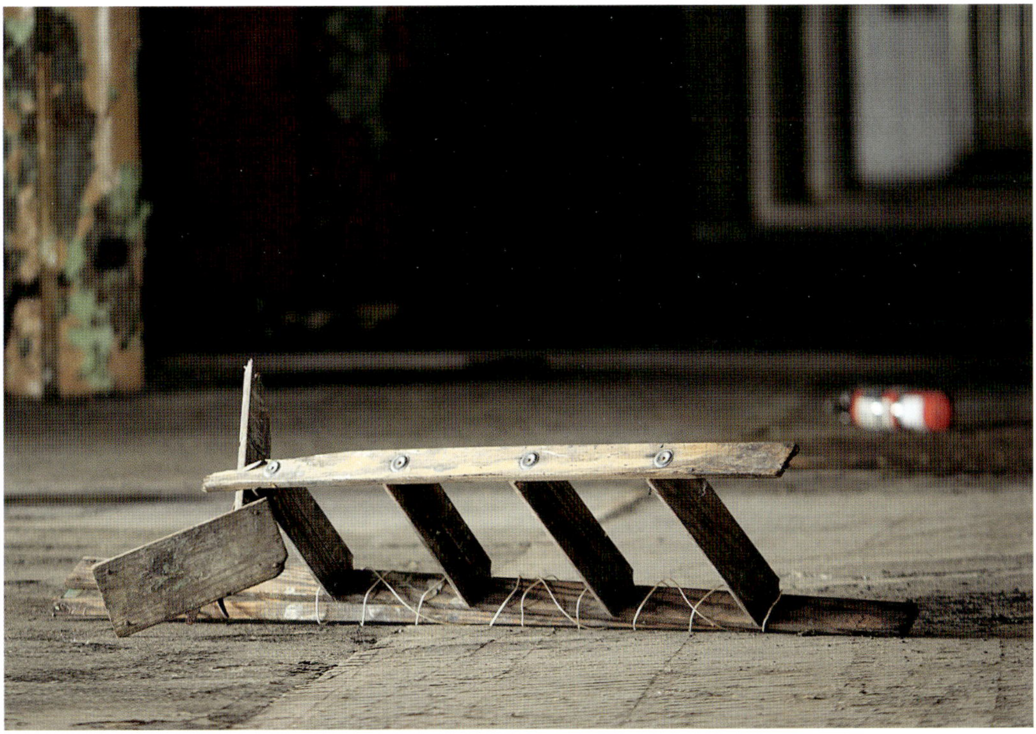

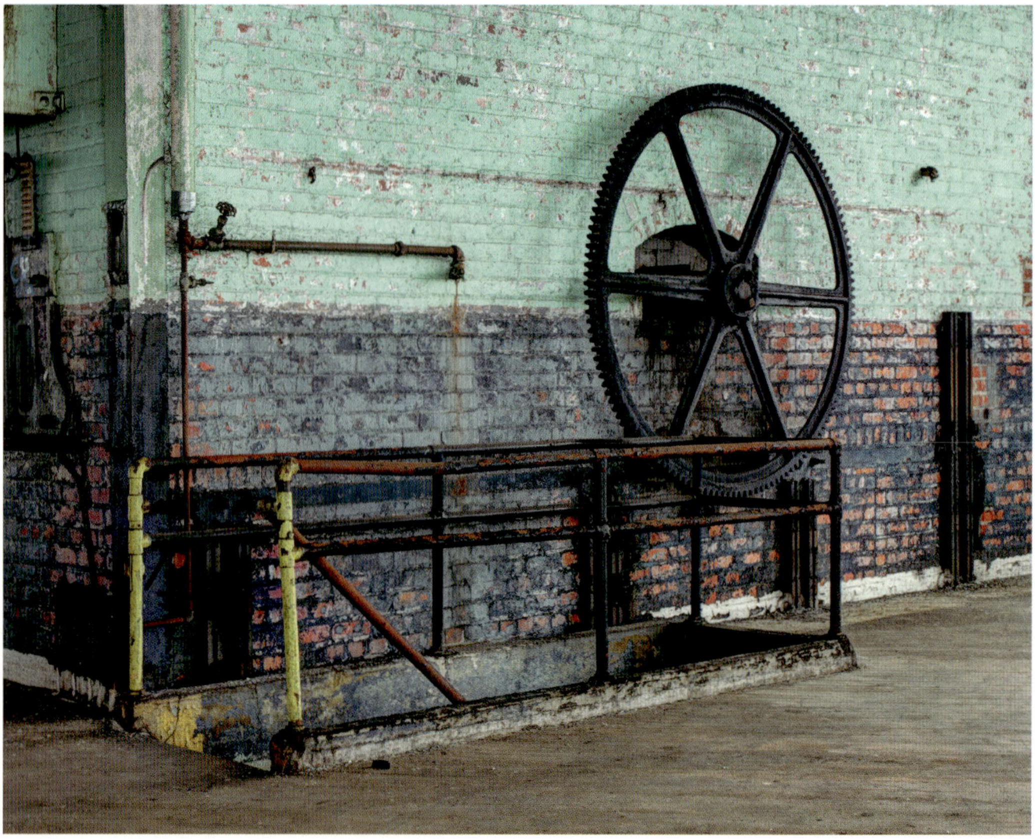

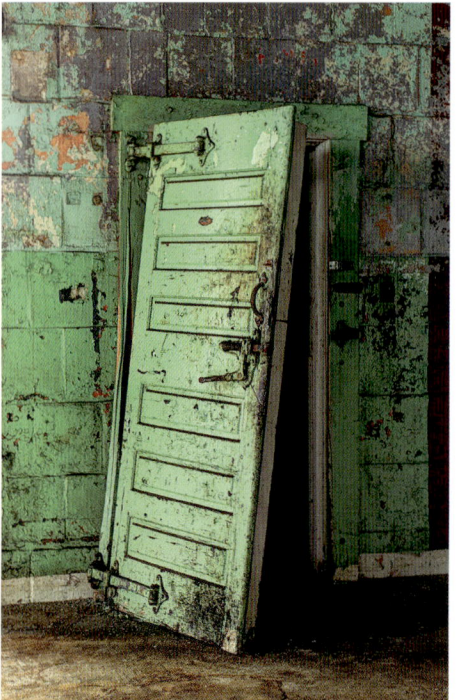

Above: The rotating crank assembly for one of the cookie ovens.

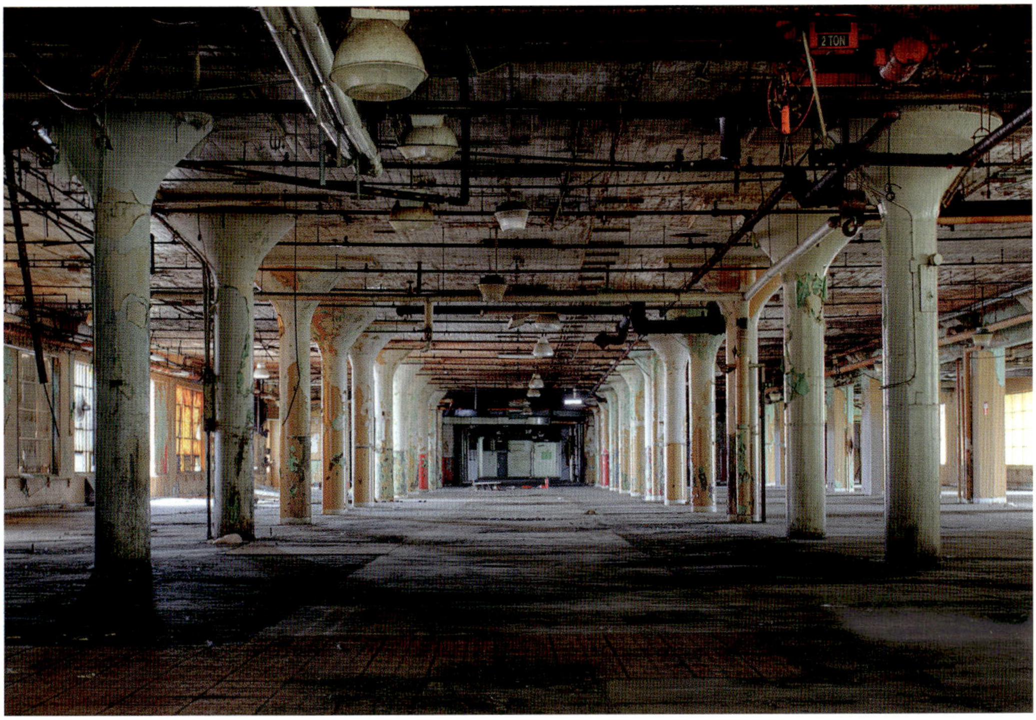

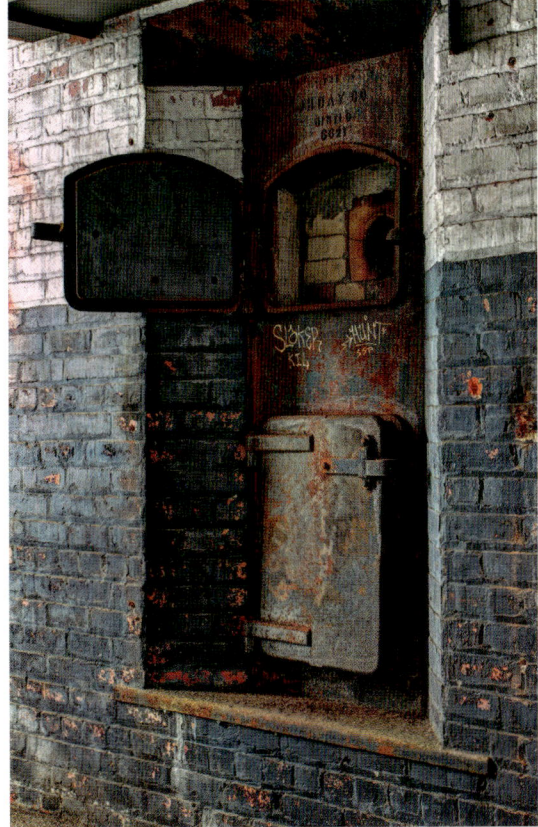

Above: The shape of these columns was common in industrial facilities constructed in the early twentieth century.

Right: These small hatches are on the exterior of the cookie ovens.

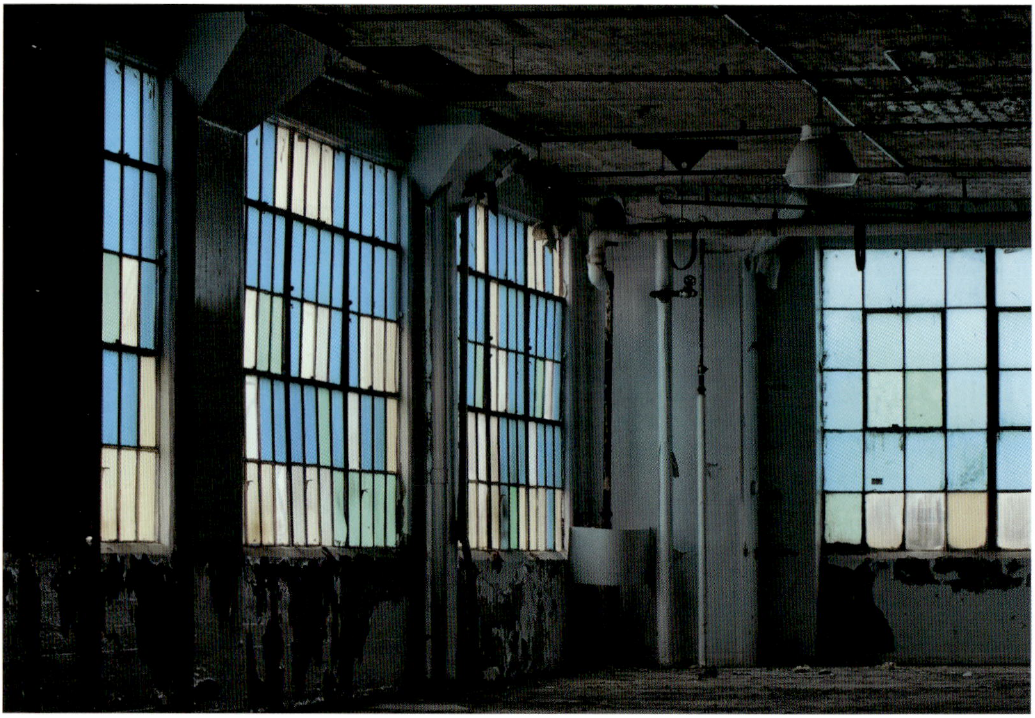

Blue windows offered some cooler light on one of the upper floors.

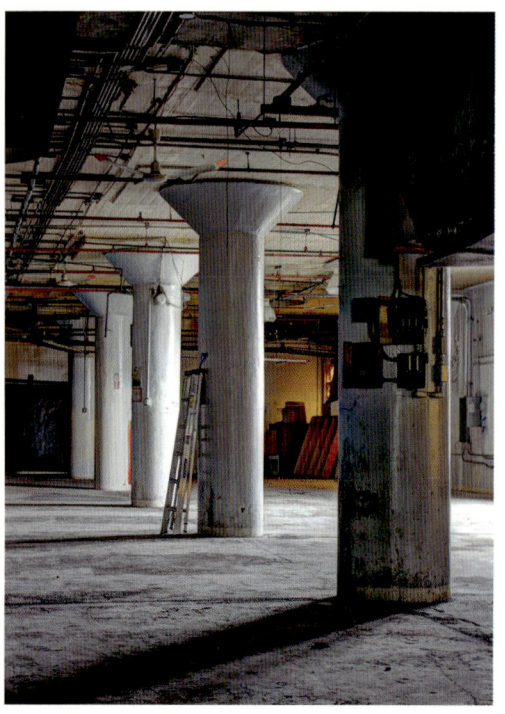

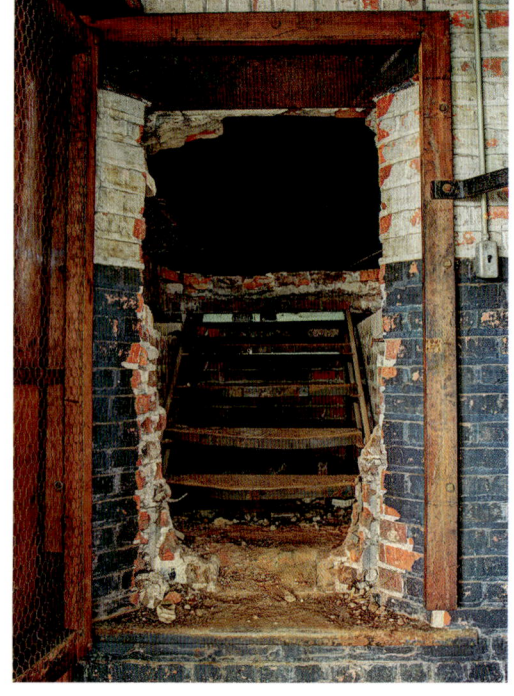

Beyond this opening lie the cookie ovens.

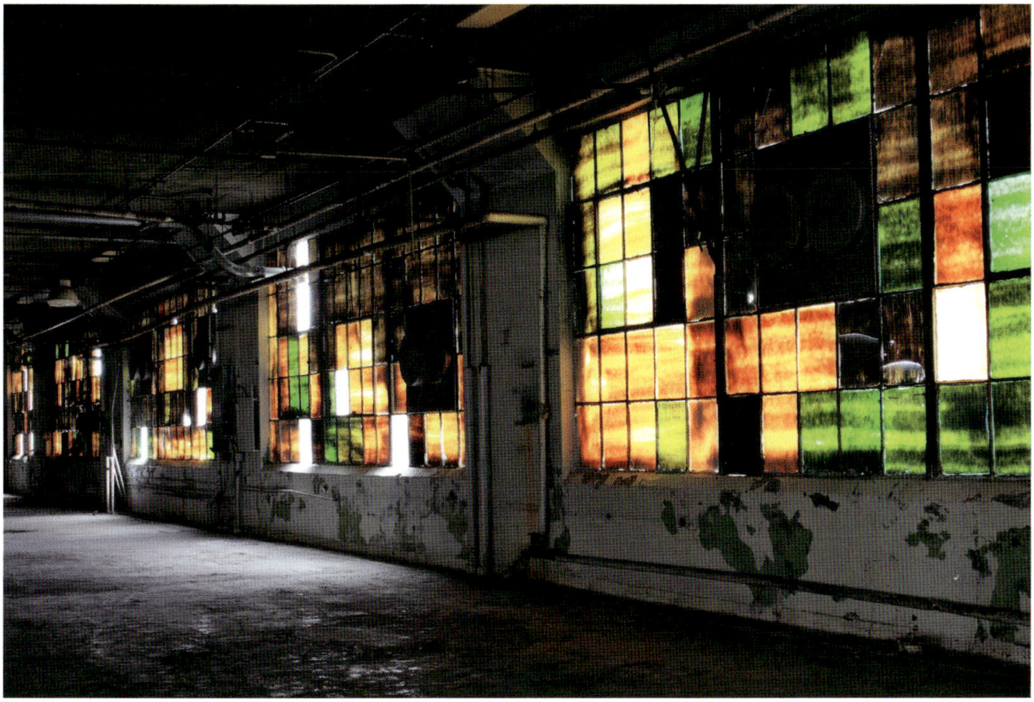

Multi-colored windows on the ground floor.

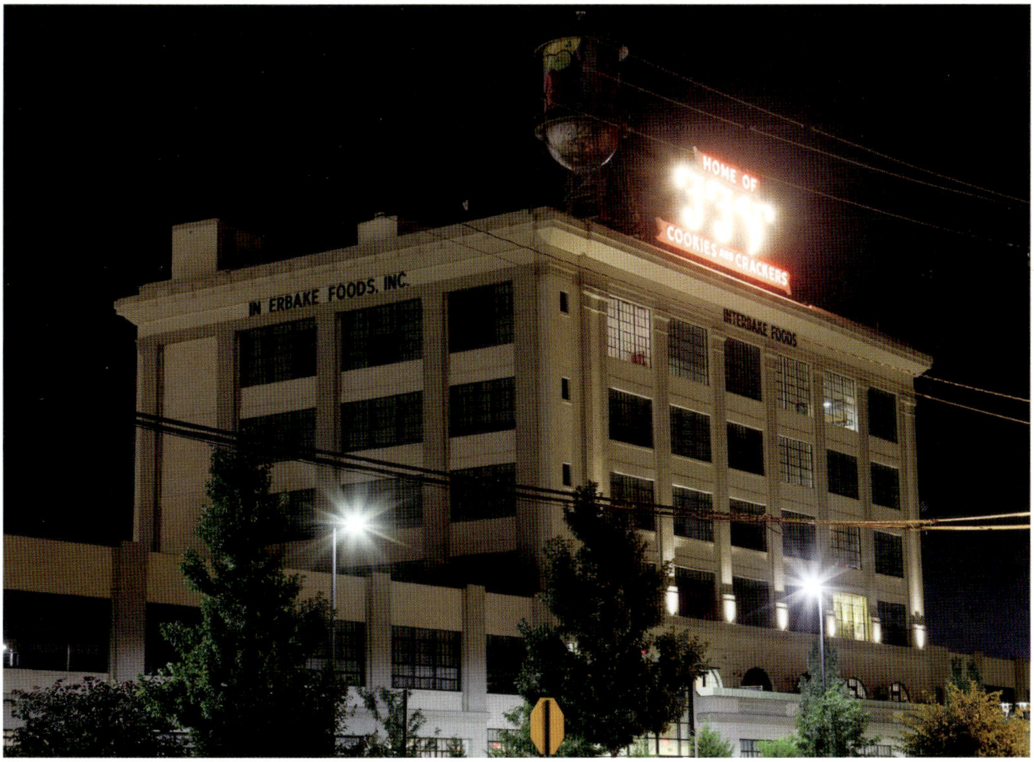

The renovated Cookie Factory Lofts in 2019.

7

FULTON GAS WORKS

Richmond, VA

Towering over Williamsburg Avenue in Richmond, Fulton Gas Works is one of the most easily visible abandoned properties in the city. Passing motorists will see the large tile letters on the brick building, which reads, "FULTON GAS WORKS." The property consists of two remaining industrial buildings, three small sheds, and the tall skeletal remains of a gas storage tank.

Producing manufactured gas out of coal was a common method of developing fuel as an urban utility in the nineteenth century. Before electricity use became widespread, manufactured gas was a commonly used system for illuminating public streetlights.

Fulton Gas Works originally started out as Richmond Municipal Gas Works, alternately referred to as Richmond Gas Works. Even though private ownership of utilities was common in the United States, Richmond Gas Works was owned and operated by the City of Richmond. The initial Richmond Gas Works facility was constructed on Cary Street in 1851. Operations were expanded to a second facility later in the 1850s, which was constructed at this Williamsburg Road site. This group of buildings was torn down and subsequently replaced with a new facility at the same location in 1925.[1] These more recent buildings are the ones which are pictured here. As a result of declining demand for gas and coal byproducts, combined with damages suffered during Hurricane Agnes, the plant closed its operations for good in 1972.[2,3]

During my visits to the property, the most striking characteristic of these gas works buildings was the extent to which they had been tagged with graffiti. This condition is to be expected on large buildings that have been vacant for nearly fifty years, and are also located in close proximity to a city center. There were also some rusted metal desks, office chairs, filing cabinets, a metal safe, and even a broken and disused eyechart. I also found documents that dated back to the 1960s and 1970s. The largest room in the main building contains the remnants of a system of retorts, pipes, condensers, and purifiers, all of which were used to manufacture and transport the gas.

There have been multiple proposals to rehabilitate this gas works facility over the last few decades, either for residential or commercial use. Unfortunately, the toxicity of the ground has proven to be a hurdle for renovation. The tar byproduct of converting coal into gas was actually once used to seal the hulls of local ships, but dock workers did not realize the carcinogenic properties of the tar at that time. This same toxic tar has leeched into the ground of Fulton Gas Works over the years, as a result of being disposed of through on-site pits and underground tanks.[4] Hopefully a reliable method of decontamination will be utilized at some point, so that this historically significant building can be put to some use once again.

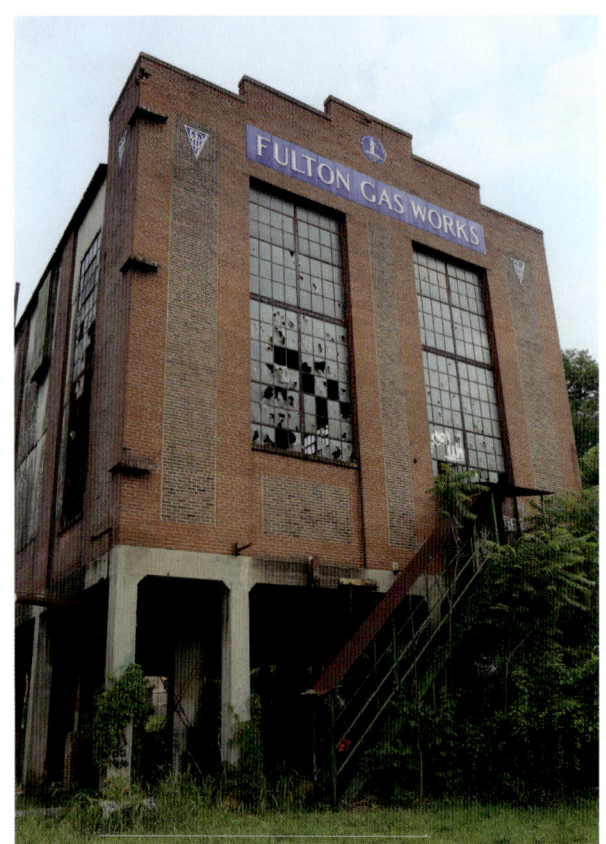

Left: This facade of broken windows and brick can be seen from a nearby road.

Below: Leftover furniture from the middle of the twentieth century.

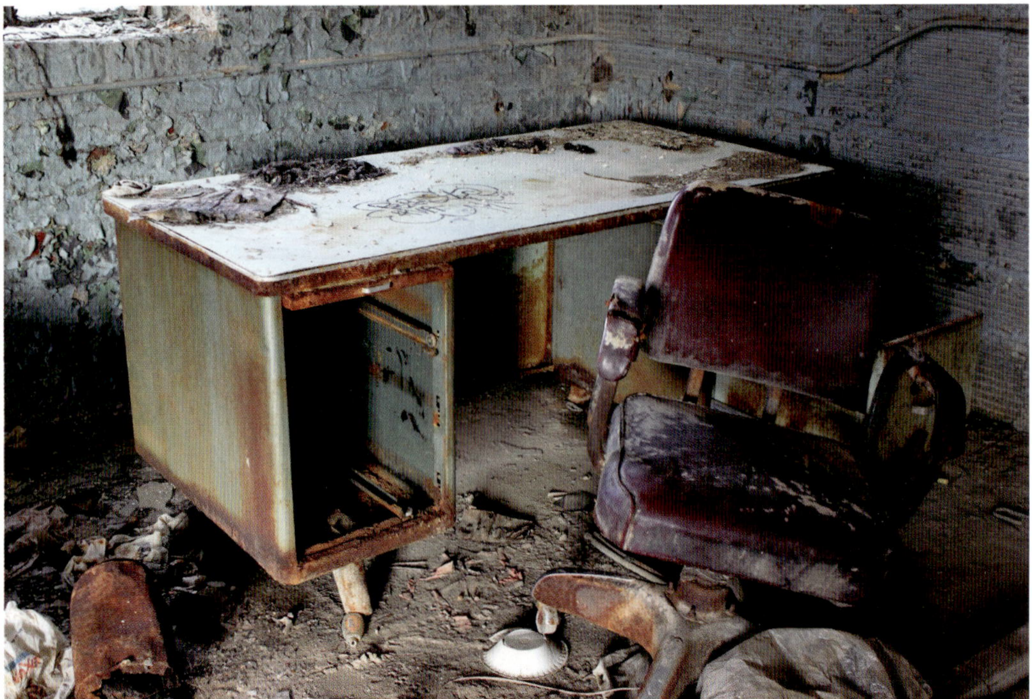

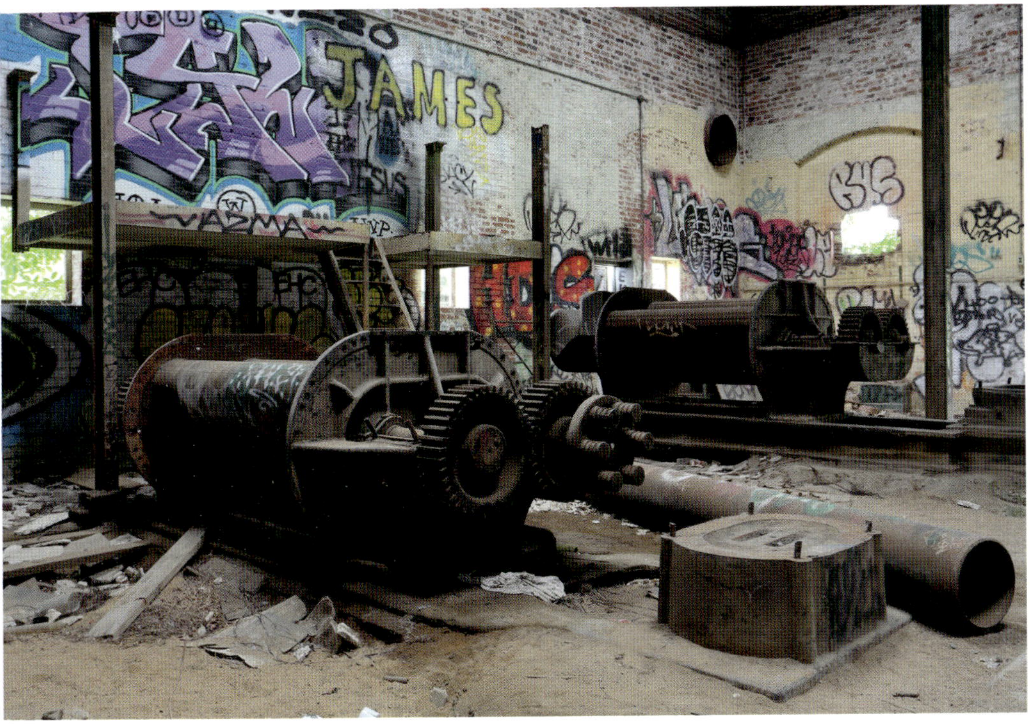

Two large compressors inside a spacious part of the complex.

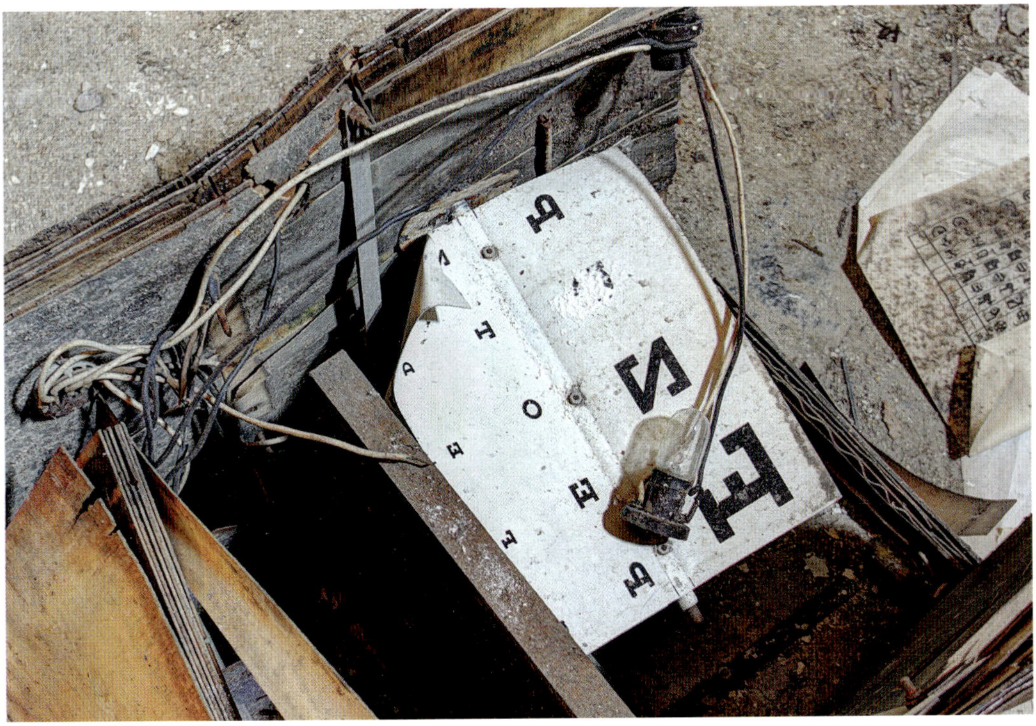

An eye exam chart was left behind.

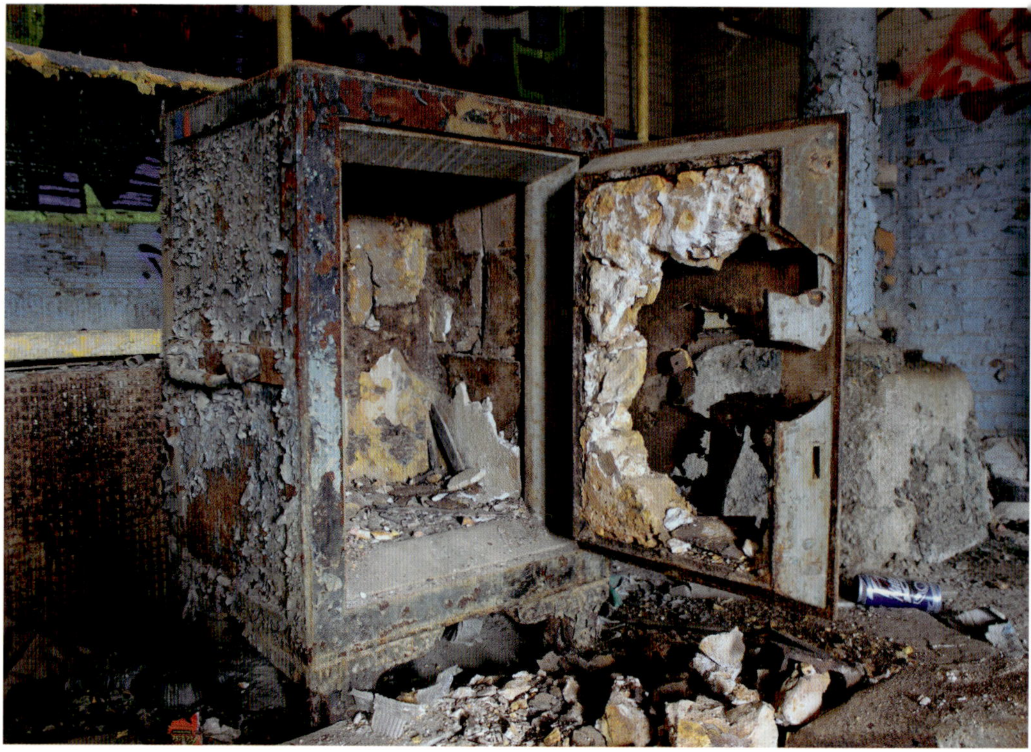

This safe has long since been emptied of its valuables.

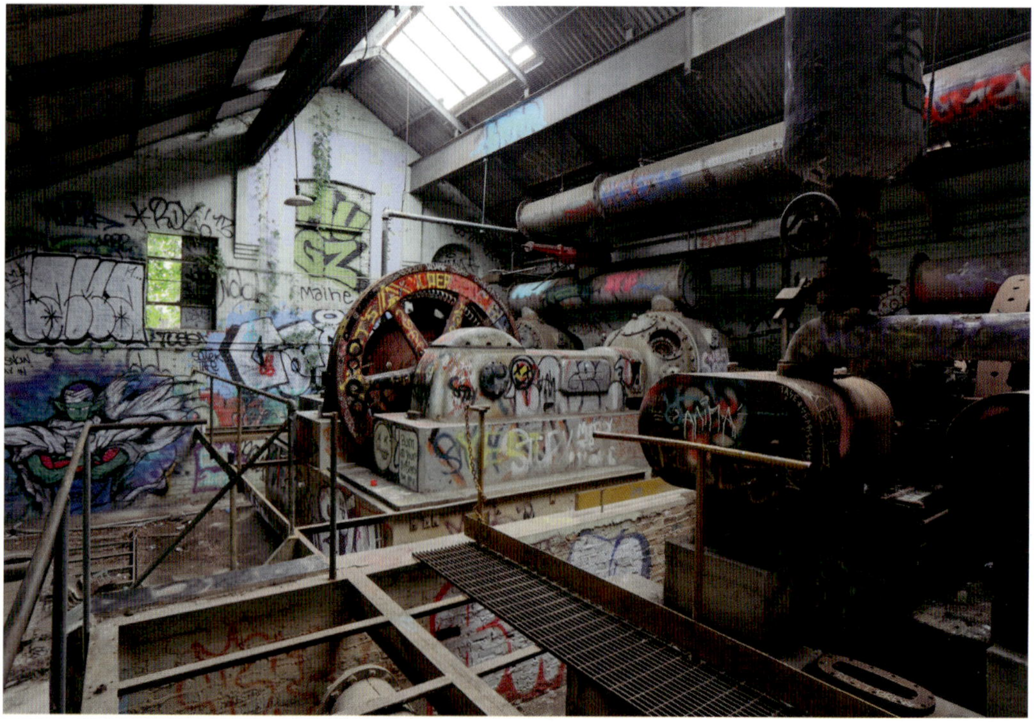

It appears that many people have explored this building since it was vacated.

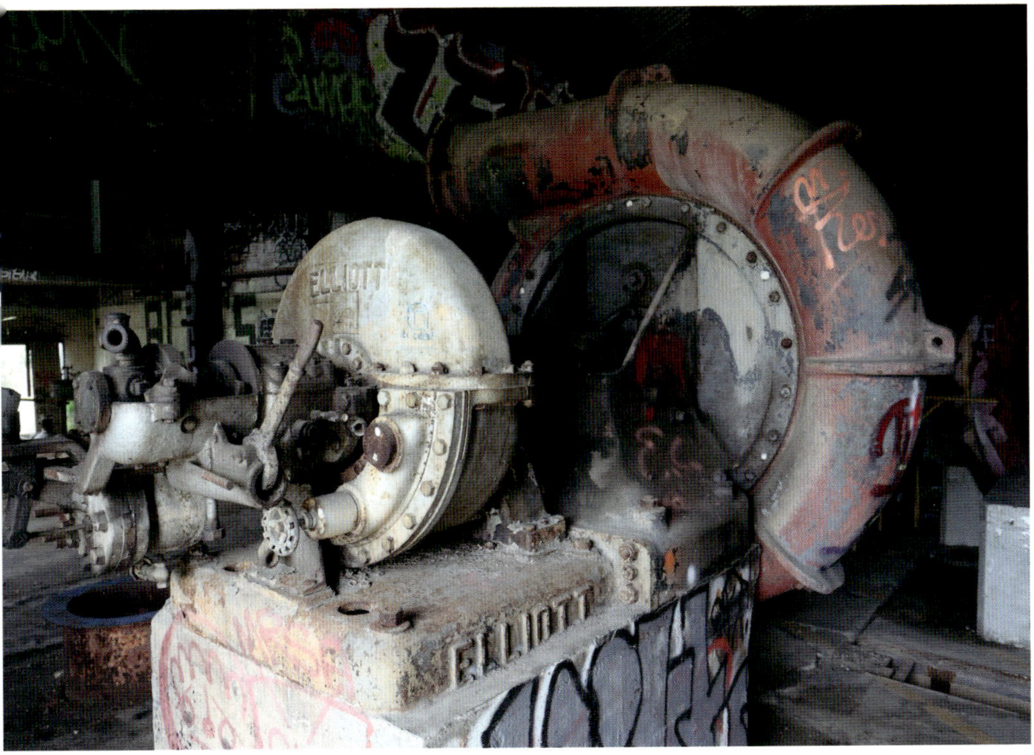

These large exhausters are about eight feet tall.

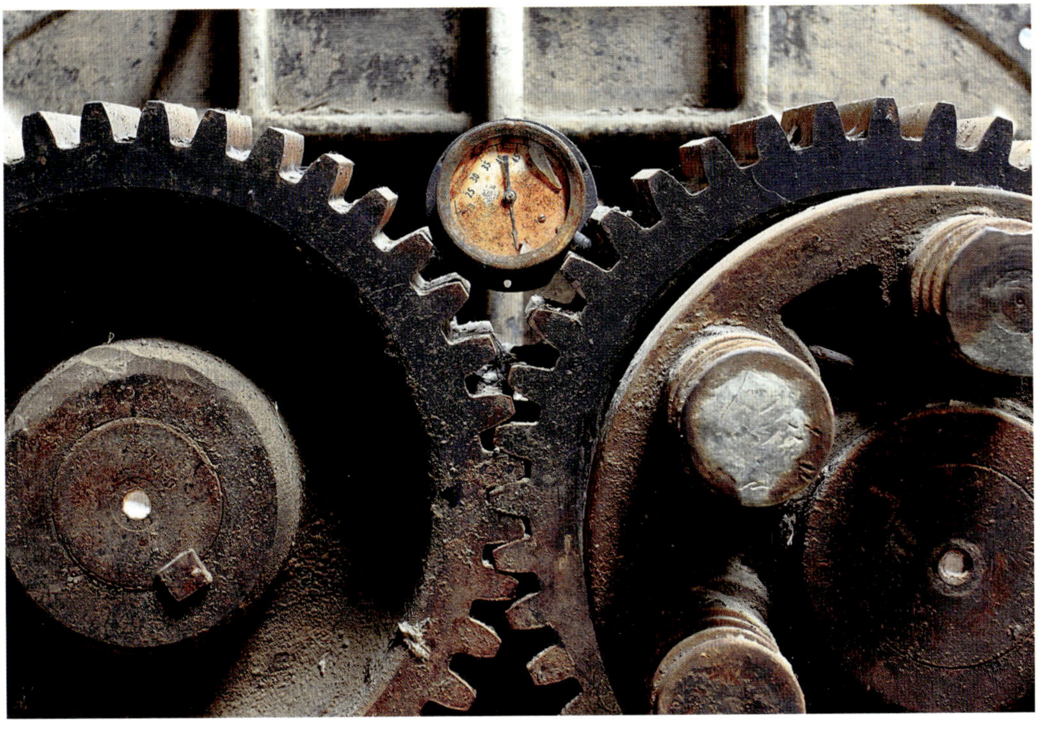

A close-up view of the gears at the end of a compressor.

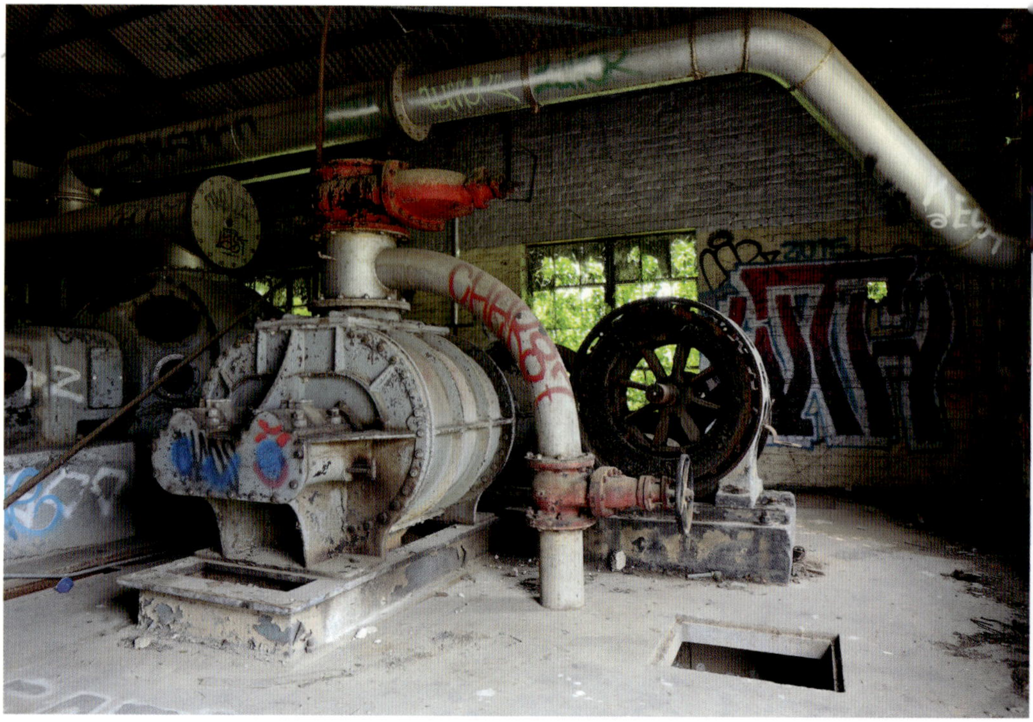

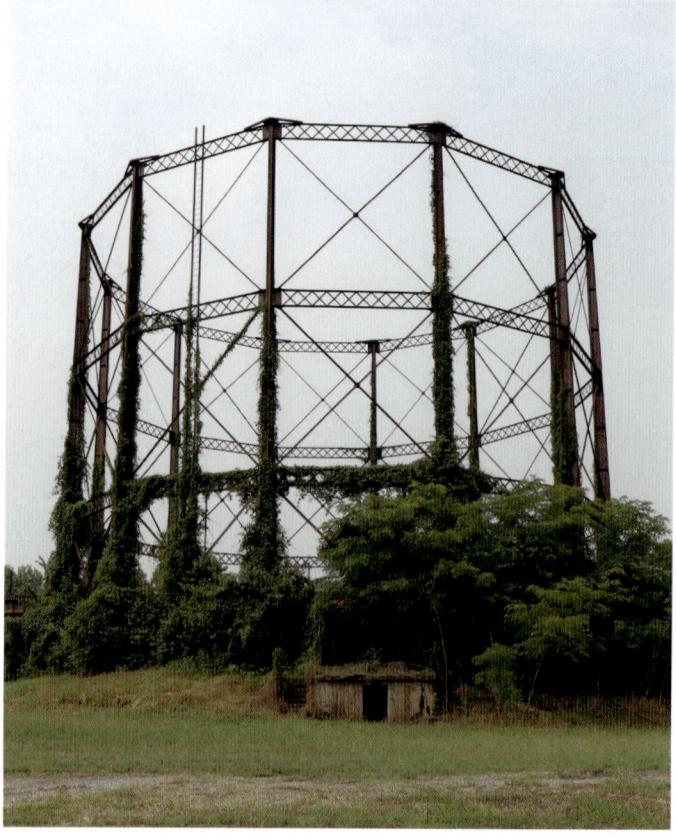

Left: This skeleton is all that remains of the large gas storage tank.

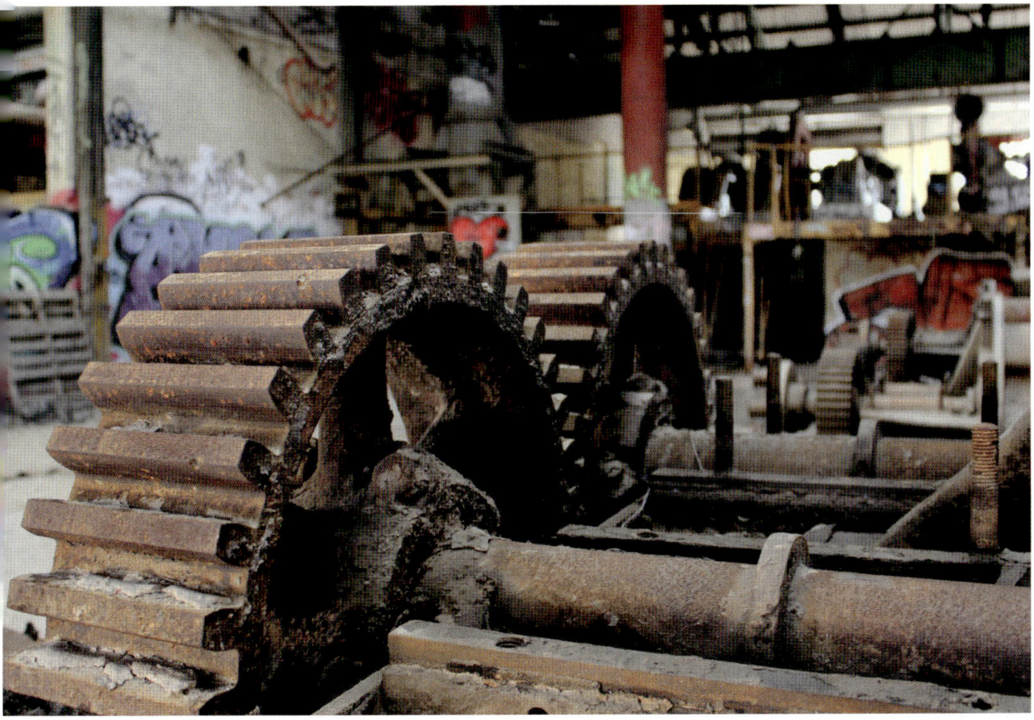

Another view from behind a compressor.

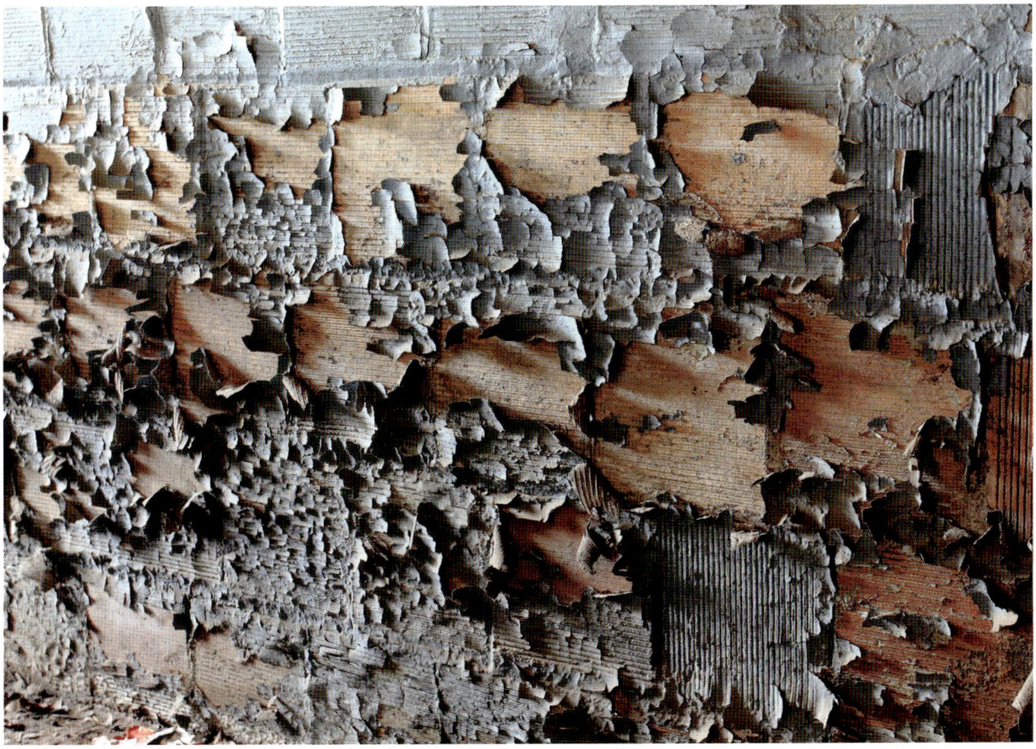

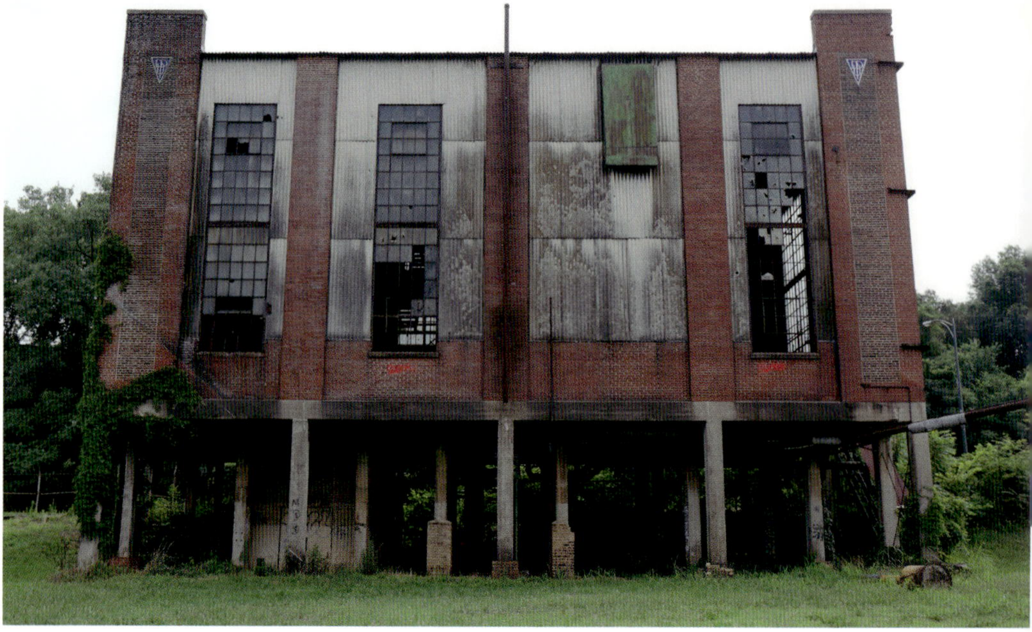

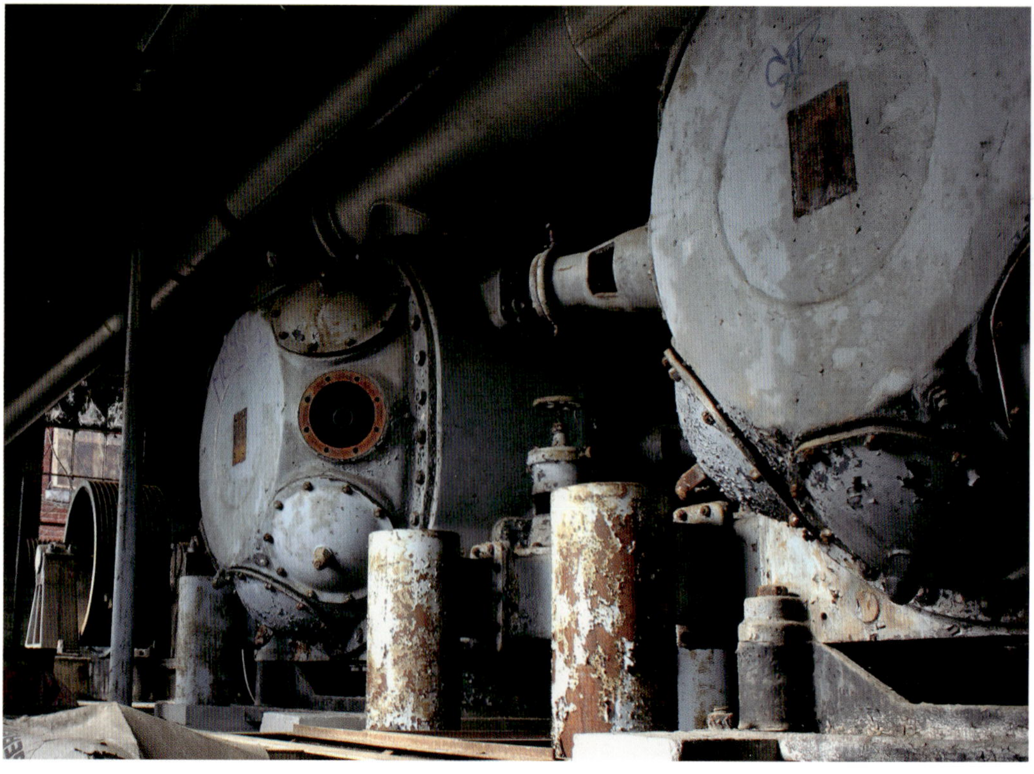

This unidentified equipment looms large in the shadows.

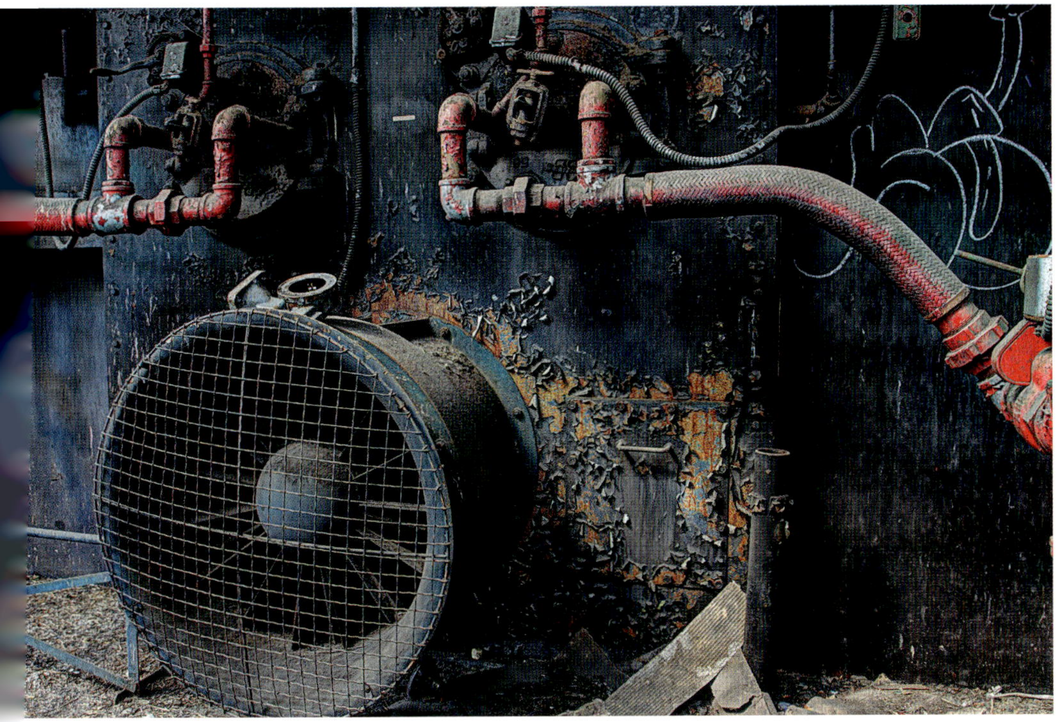

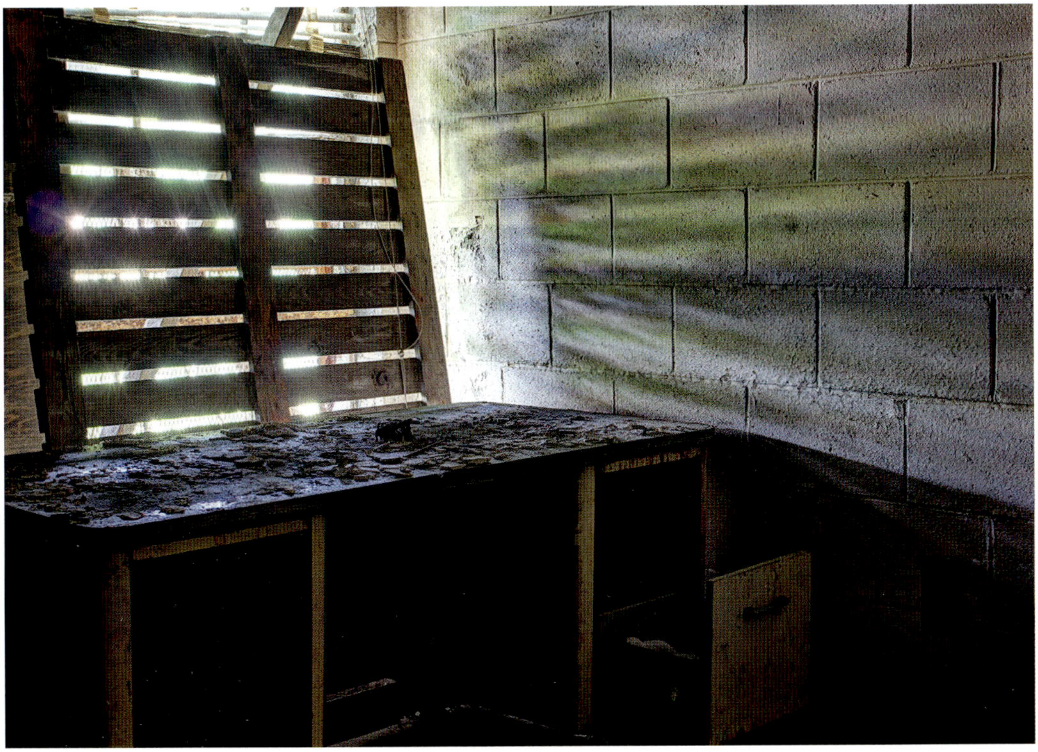

Sunlight coming through some pallet wood.

8

CREIGHTON ROAD FARMHOUSE

MECHANICSVILLE, VA

Farmhouses like this one in Mechanicsville have a tendency to slow down the perception of time. While exploring this house, it is easy to imagine sitting on the front porch on a cool summer evening, watching the sun as it sets, and waiting for the fireflies to come out. The long driveway means that you know who is visiting long before they even get out of their vehicle. Or perhaps, before they even get off their horse. This house was built in 1890, so it has witnessed quite a few changes in the world since it was constructed.

My favorite feature of this house was the kitchen. The contrasting pale yellow and white checkerboard-patterned cabinets were straight out of the 1960s. The window trim and wall trim were also color-matched with the same shade of yellow. Keeping the theme going, some of the stairway bannisters and radiators were painted yellow as well. The mid-century General Electric kitchen stove appeared to be from the same era as the cabinets.

As with many rural houses, there was no evidence of vandalism in this house. Besides some paint peeling on the walls and ceiling, and a few areas where the plaster was deteriorated, this house was more or less intact. It is hard to know for sure, but I like to think that the right buyer will come along and renovate this house someday. I am crossing my fingers that they will restore the kitchen in the same mid-century fashion!

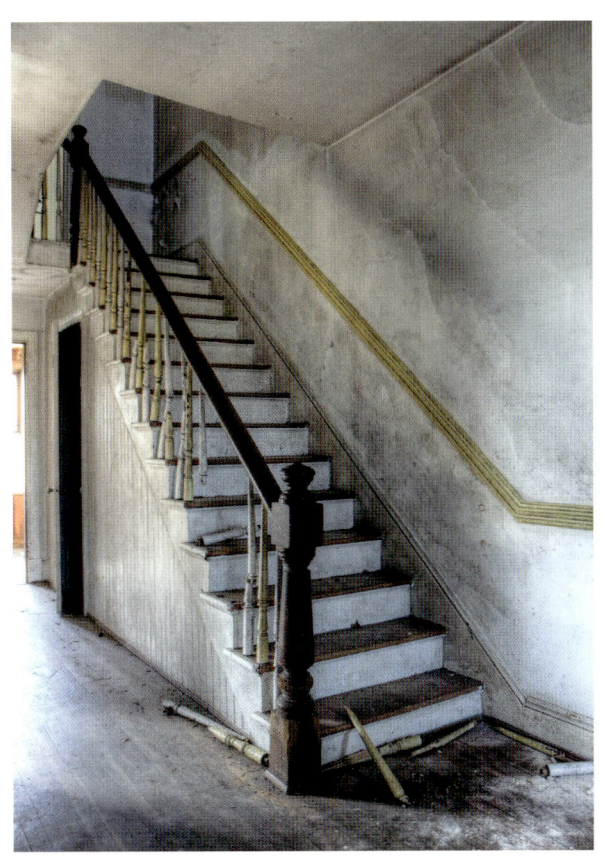

Right: It's a mystery how walls can get this dirty.

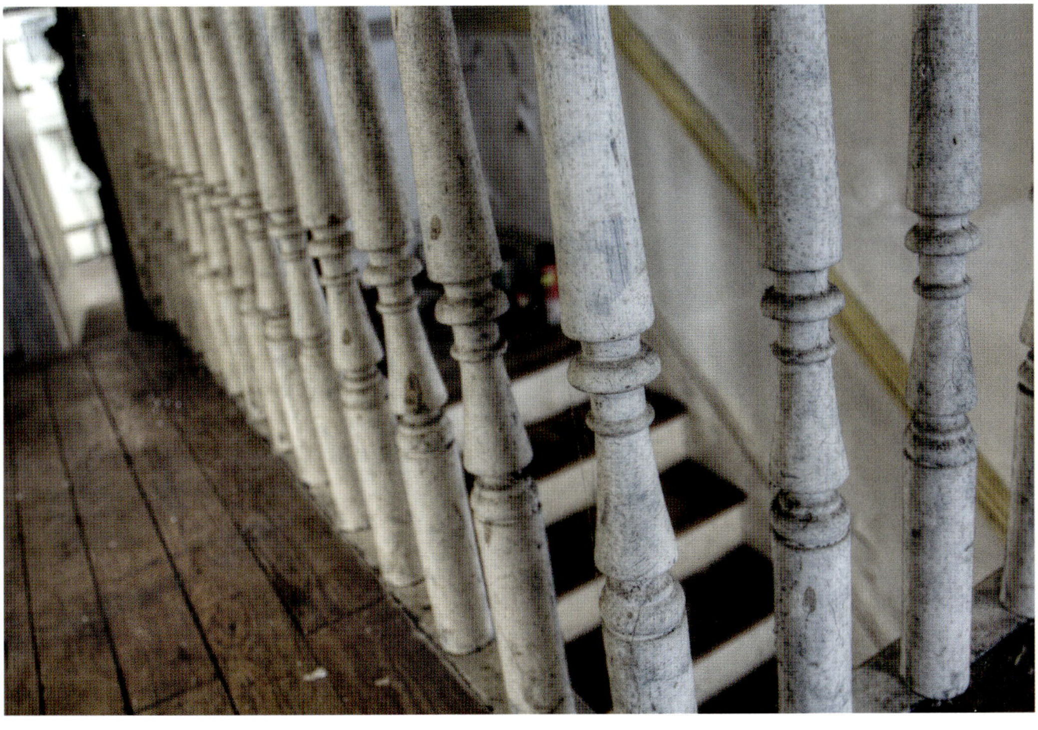

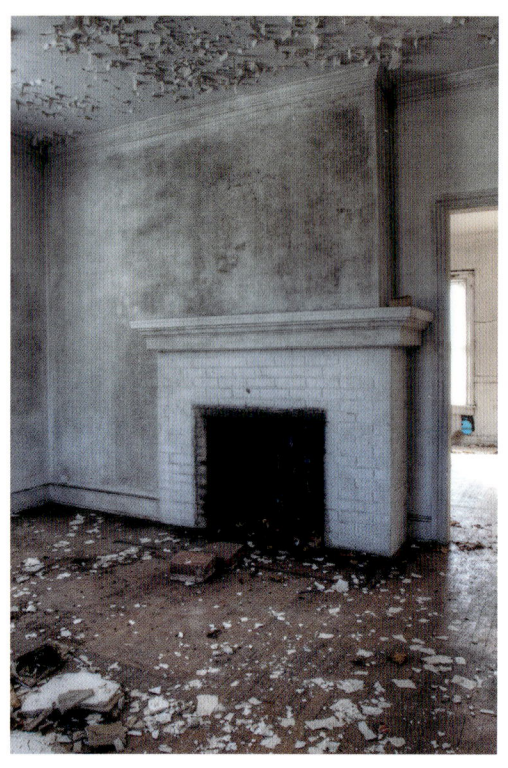
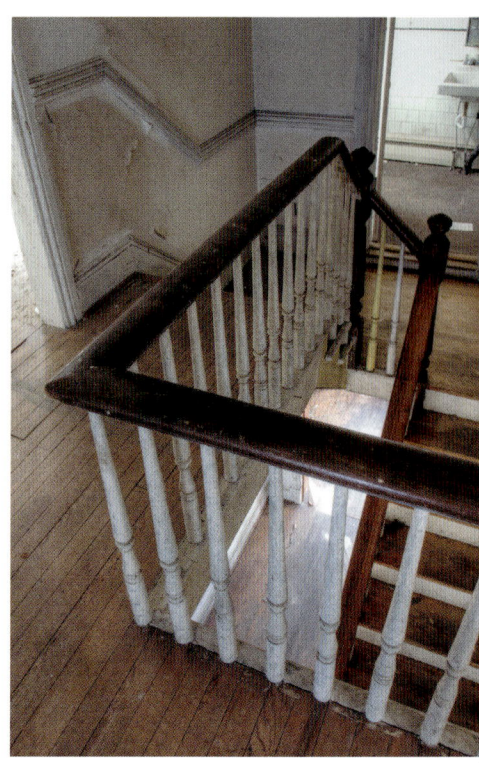

More dirty walls and paint loss.

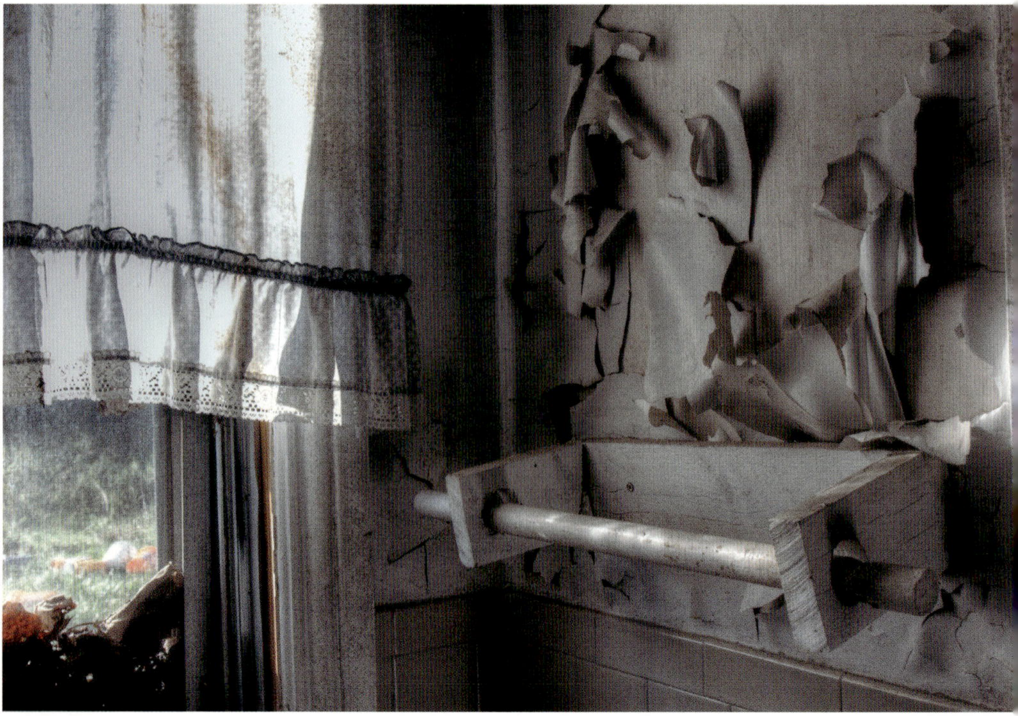

A towel rack inside one of the bathrooms.

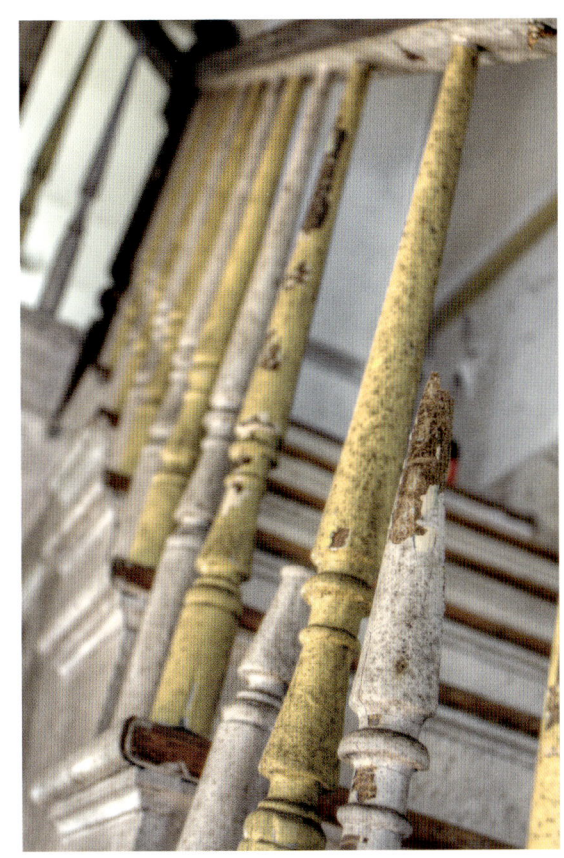

Below: This farmhouse kitchen is straight out of the mid-twentieth century.

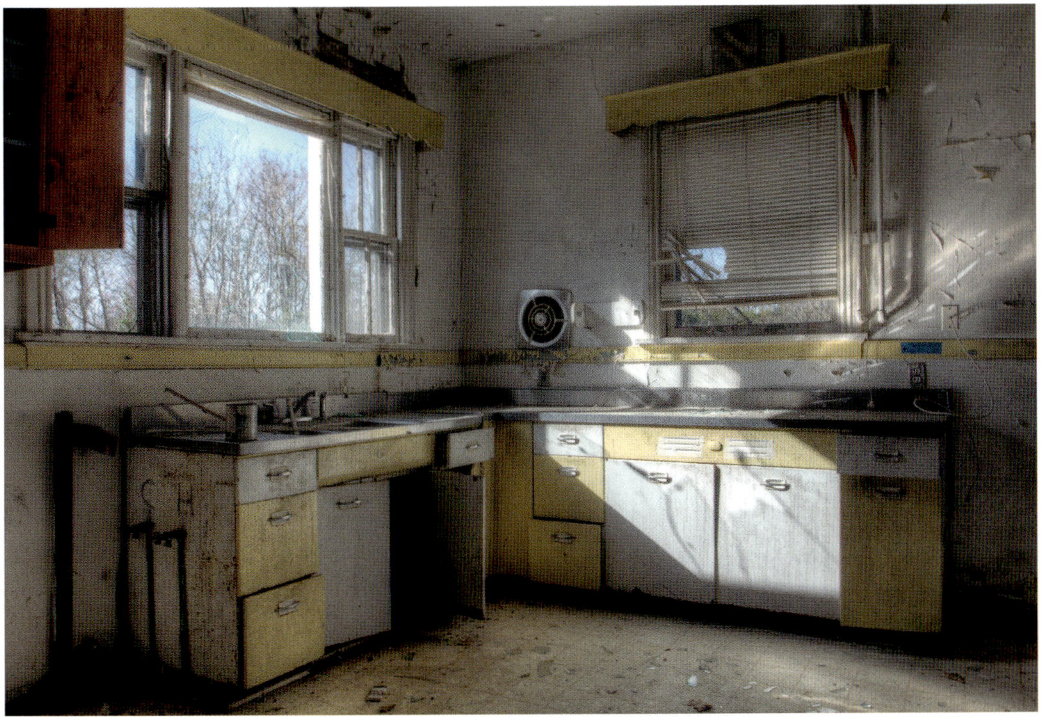

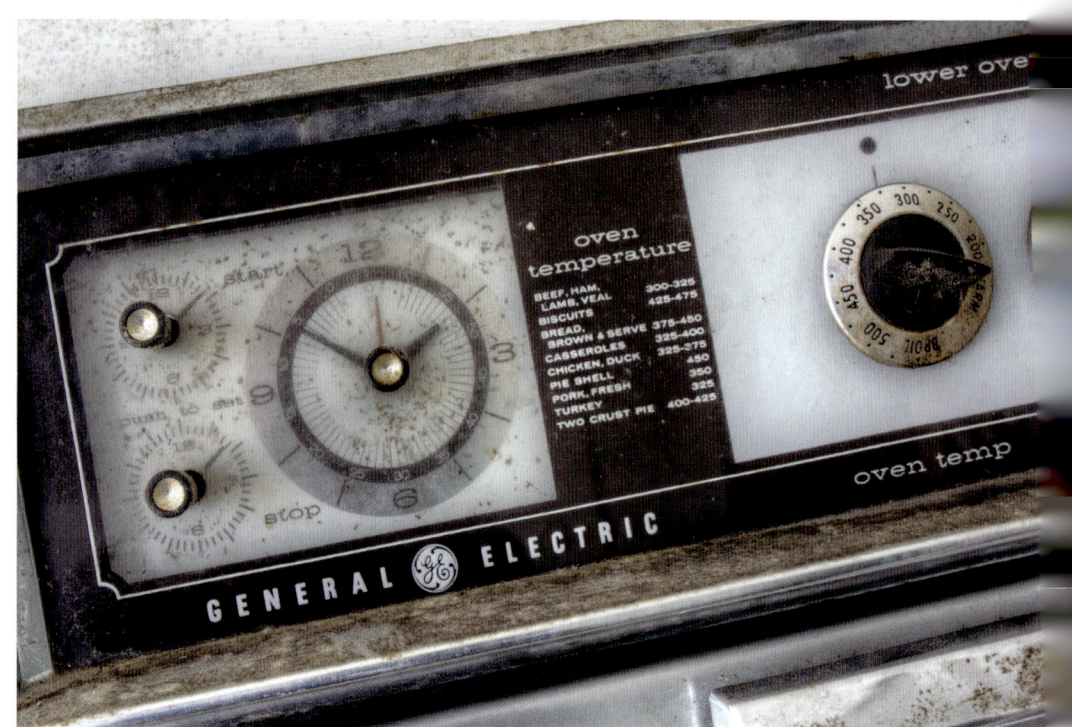

Above: Vintage oven with convenient temperature guide.

Left: A crumbling wall inside one of the bedrooms.

Below: Close-up view of a kitchen drawer handle.

9

CENTRAL NATIONAL BANK

RICHMOND, VA

The Central National Bank building is the most architecturally impressive building that I have ever photographed. With an Art Deco style that is very much in line with its 1929 construction date, this skyscraper was the tallest building in Richmond for several decades.

The story of Central National Bank began in 1911, when a group of small business owners established their first bank branch at 307 East Broad Street. They made some waves in the banking industry when they started offering bank accounts to women. These accounts were even managed by the bank's first female employee. Authorization to construct a new bank building was approved by the Board of Directors in 1928. Originally, they planned for the building to be ten stories, but this was later increased to twelve, then fifteen, and ultimately twenty-four stories. Construction of the new bank building at 219 East Broad Street began in 1929, and was completed in 1930. The new bank building was an immediate success, and by 1936, Central National Bank had amassed a total of $18 million in assets.[1]

Interestingly enough, two members of the Schwarzschild family have served as presidents of Central National Bank. William H. Schwarzschild took the helm as President in 1919, and his son, W. Harry Schwarzschild, Jr., was elected for the position in 1949. This is the same family that built a successful local jewelry business, and theirs is one of the most easily recognized names in Richmond.[2]

Design of the Central National Bank building was completed by celebrated architect John Eberson. The Art Deco style includes heavy use of geometric and angular forms, and the expression of this design style in skyscrapers reflects linearity, verticality, and sleekness. The verticality of the building was enhanced through brick pilasters between the windows, which taper as they get closer to the top, and also through darkened panels above and below the windows. The impression is further enhanced by the tapered silhouette in the upper half of the building.[3]

Entry into the main banking hall is accessed through large brass doors, beneath a massive arched window. This entrance is surrounded on the exterior by an intricate three-story arch, carved out of the limestone and granite base of the building. Upon entering the main banking hall, you are greeted with a degree of ornamentation and design that may be unrivaled by any other building in Richmond. The curved 40-foot ceiling is richly decorated with colorful plaster designs, carved in a relief over the entire surface. Traveling down the center of this lavish ceiling is a repeating pattern of floral medallions, and these are flanked by symmetrical recessed geometrical patterns. There are rows of windows running down both sides of the banking hall, reaching the same height as the main entrance window, but only the windows on the eastern side of the hall are facing exterior light. A series of columns run down opposite sides of the hall, and they are decorated with ornate molded plaster corbels. Though dirty and obscured from disuse, I could still make out the detail in the patterned terrazzo floors. Sadly, I witnessed some deterioration on the intricate plaster ceiling panels in the banking hall. This was likely caused by the many years of heat and cold wreaking havoc on this building, as a building without climate control is bound to crumble more rapidly.

Some of these photos show an adjacent building, the three-story Broad-Grace Arcade. This portion of the structure was previously occupied by an interior stretch of shops, which wrapped around the skyscraper, and reached from Broad Street to Grace Street. However, this arcade building was purchased by Central National Bank in the 1970s, and it was converted into a personal banking center.[4]

A spectacular find on a lower level of this building was the gold bank vault door. There was a special sort of contrast happening on this door, as the exterior mechanisms were heavily rusted, but the sealed interior looks immaculate. I have seen a few vault doors in old bank buildings, but this was easily the most ornate one I have come across. I found some evidence that the geometric Art Deco style was extended to the visible interior gears of the vault door.

Over the years, this building has been affiliated with several company names. In 1978, Fidelity American Bank merged with Central National Bank to form Commonwealth Banks. The following year, this company was renamed to Central Fidelity Bank. After Central Fidelity Bank was acquired by Wachovia Bank in 1998, the building briefly operated as a Wachovia Bank branch. Commercial operations in this building ceased when Wachovia vacated in 2000, and it remained vacant for many years.[5] A developer has since purchased the building, with the intent of refurbishing the building and converting it into apartments. It has been renamed as the Deco at CNB Building. The apartment project has been completed, and the first tenants moved into the building in 2016. This building has been a spectacular architectural contribution to Richmond, and it is wonderful for the city to have it renovated and put back to use once again.

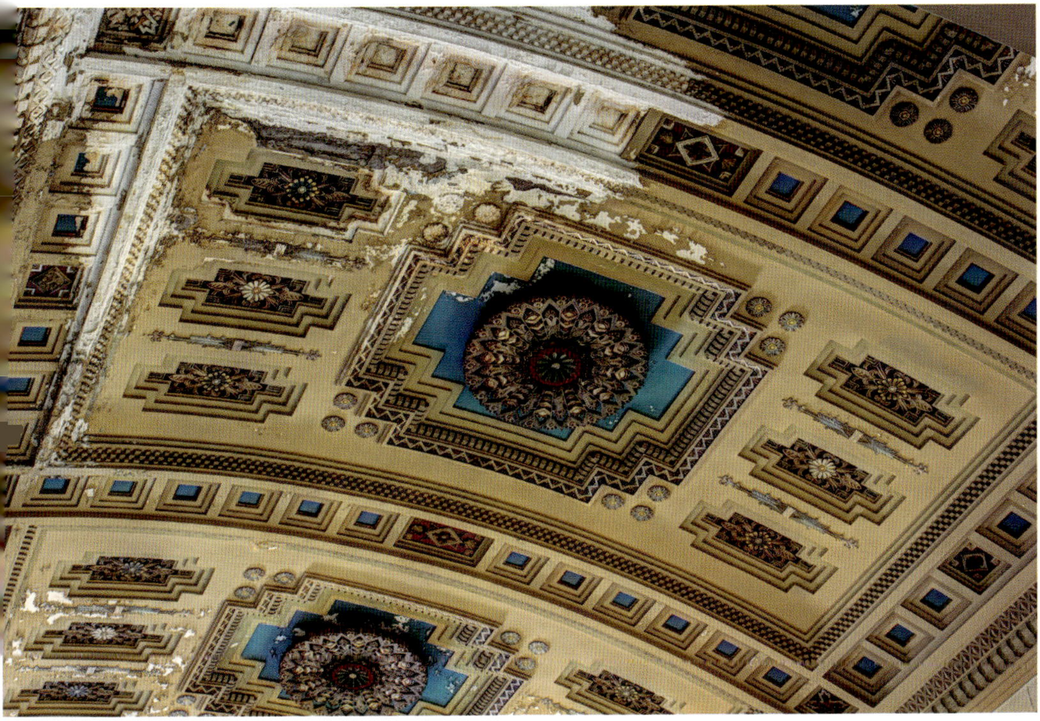

Extremely intricate details in the ceiling of the main banking hall.

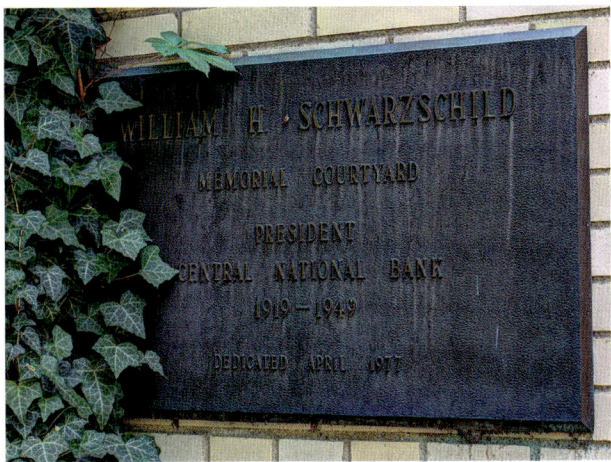

This plaque is posted in a courtyard on the building exterior.

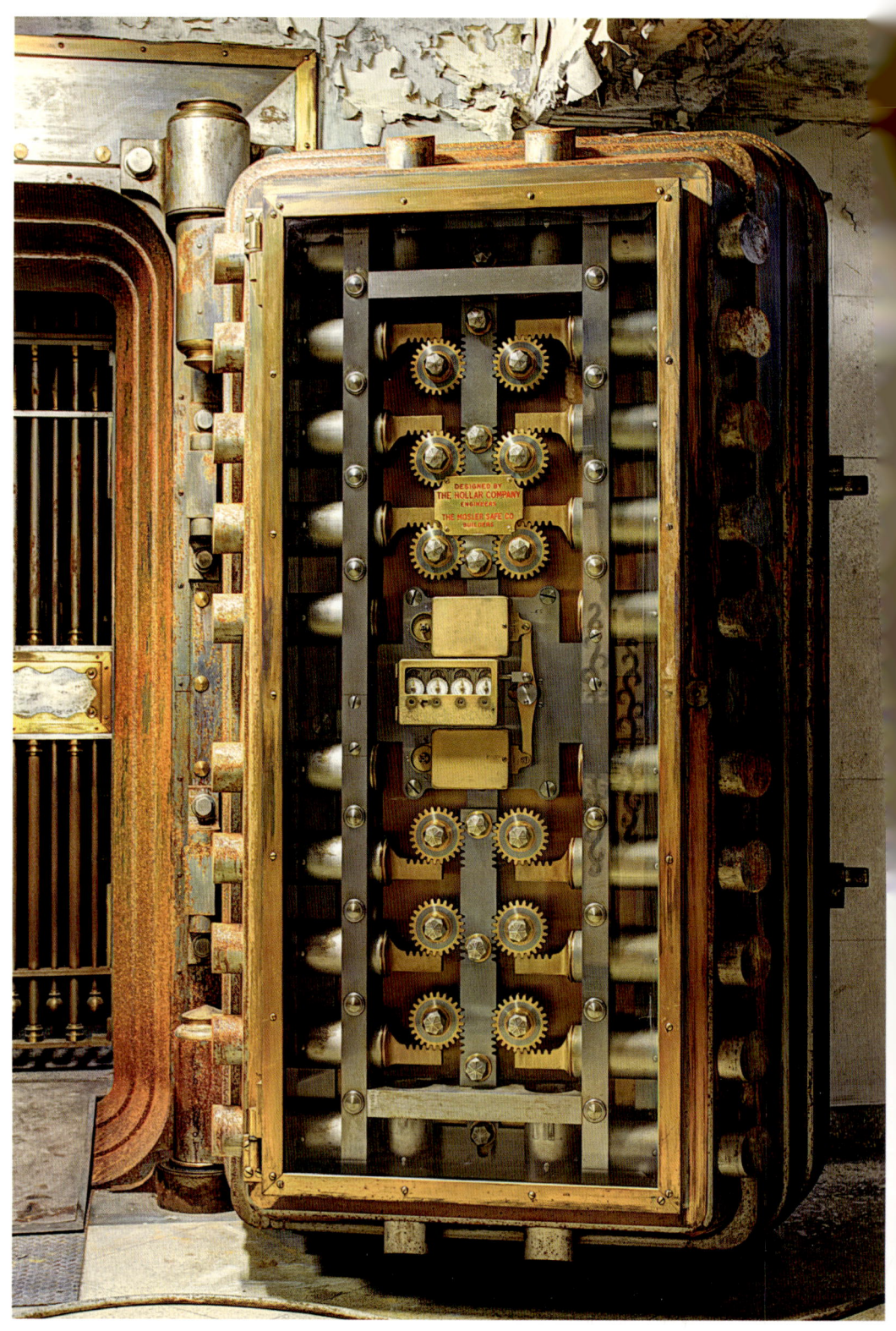

This gold-colored bank vault door was the highlight of this building.

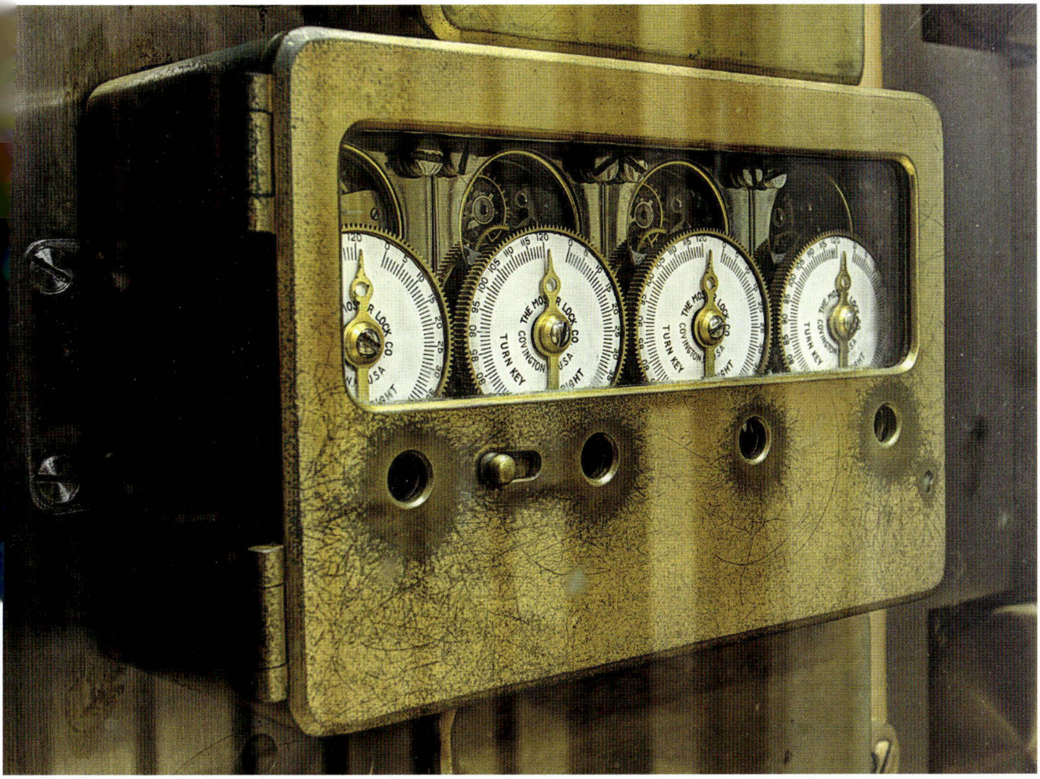

Above: The interior components of the vault door are sealed and untouched by rust.

Right: It's amazing to think that these vault door components were likely over eighty years old.

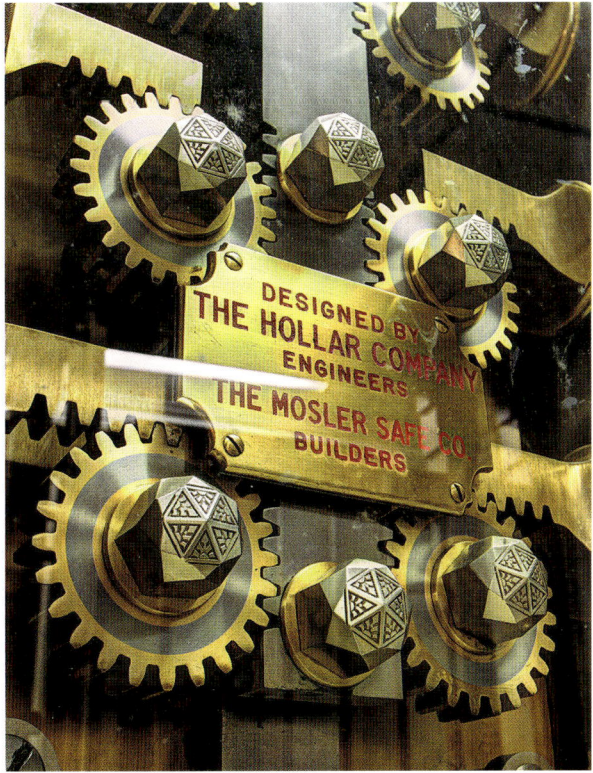

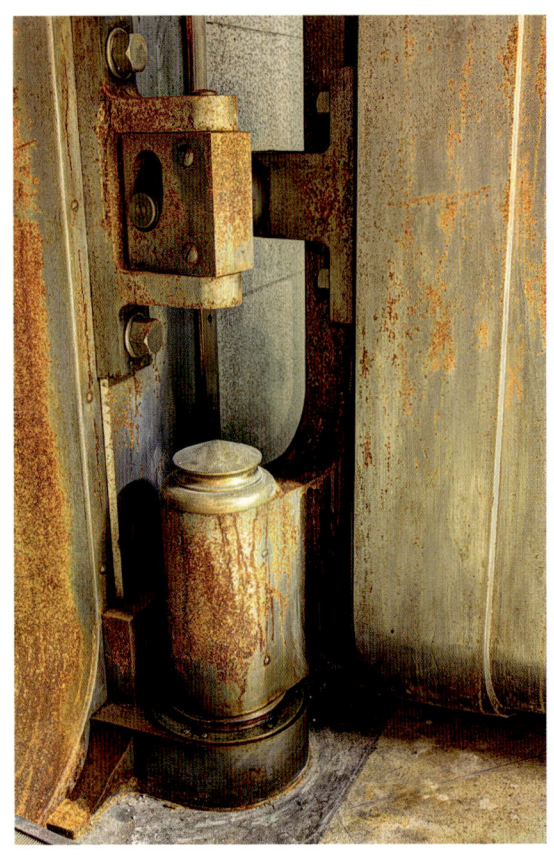

These are the large hinges on the bank vault door.

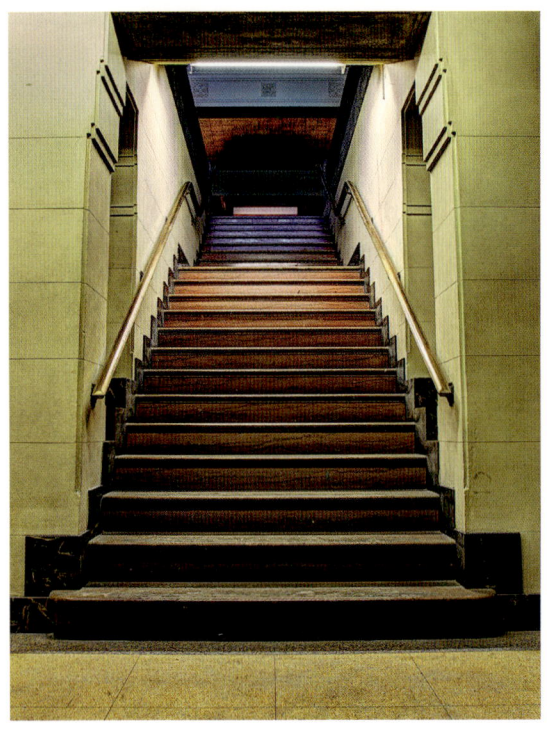

The view up the basement stairwell from the vault door.

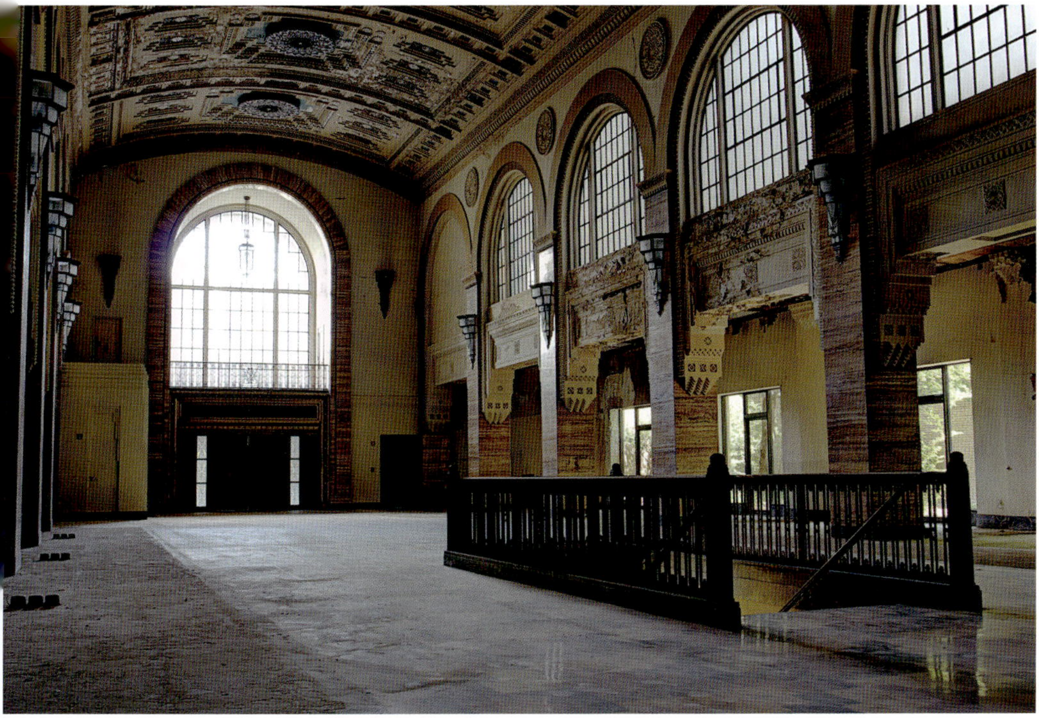

Above: A view of the extremely ornate main banking hall.

Right: This view of the basement stairwell was taken from a second-story balcony, overlooking the main banking hall.

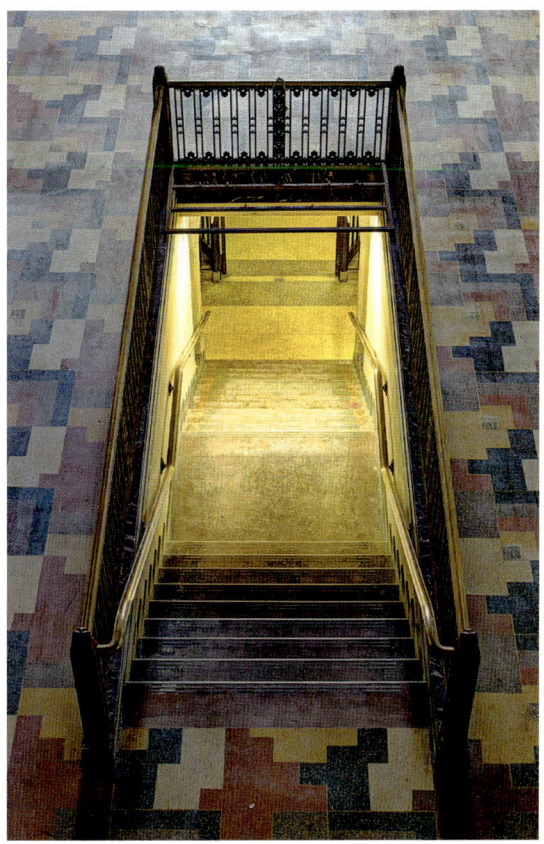

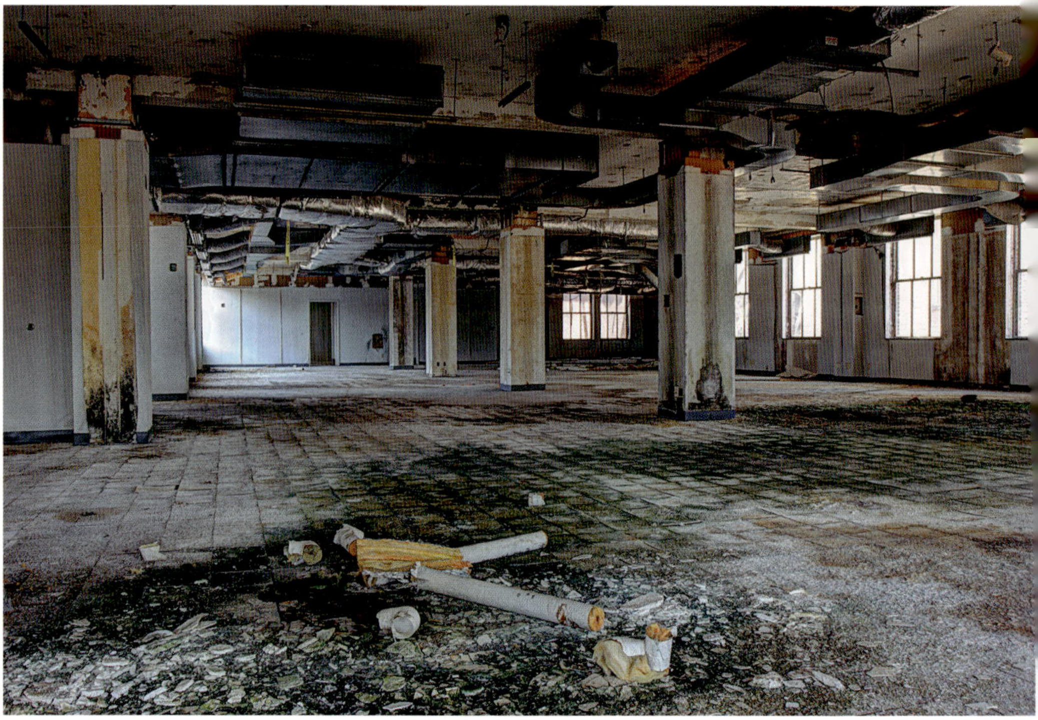

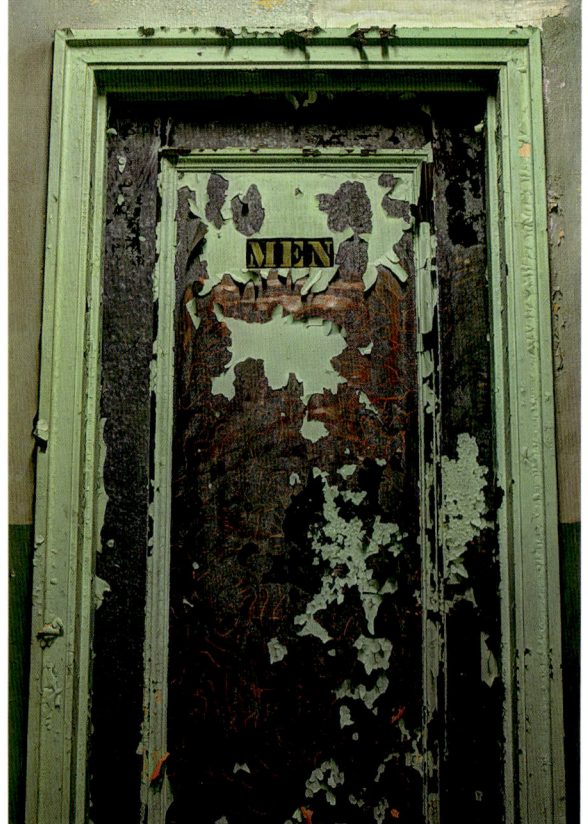

Above: Crumbled insulation in one of the floors of the arcade building, adjacent to the skyscraper.

Left: A colorful men's room door in an upper floor of the skyscraper.

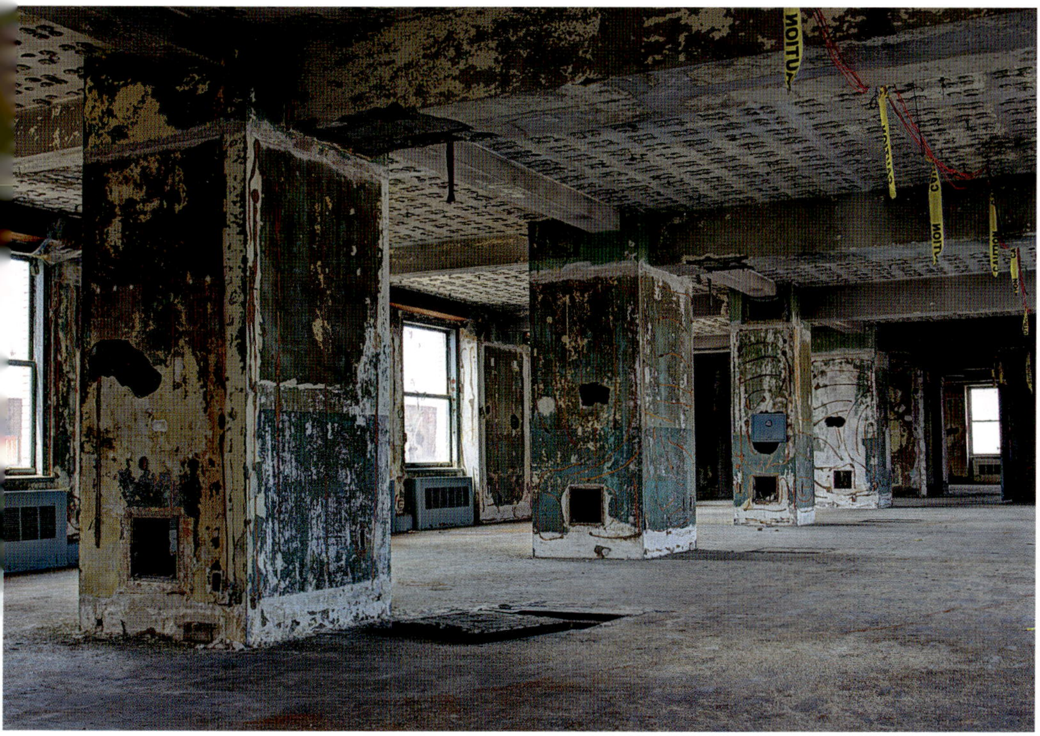

Columns inside one of the upper floors of the skyscraper.

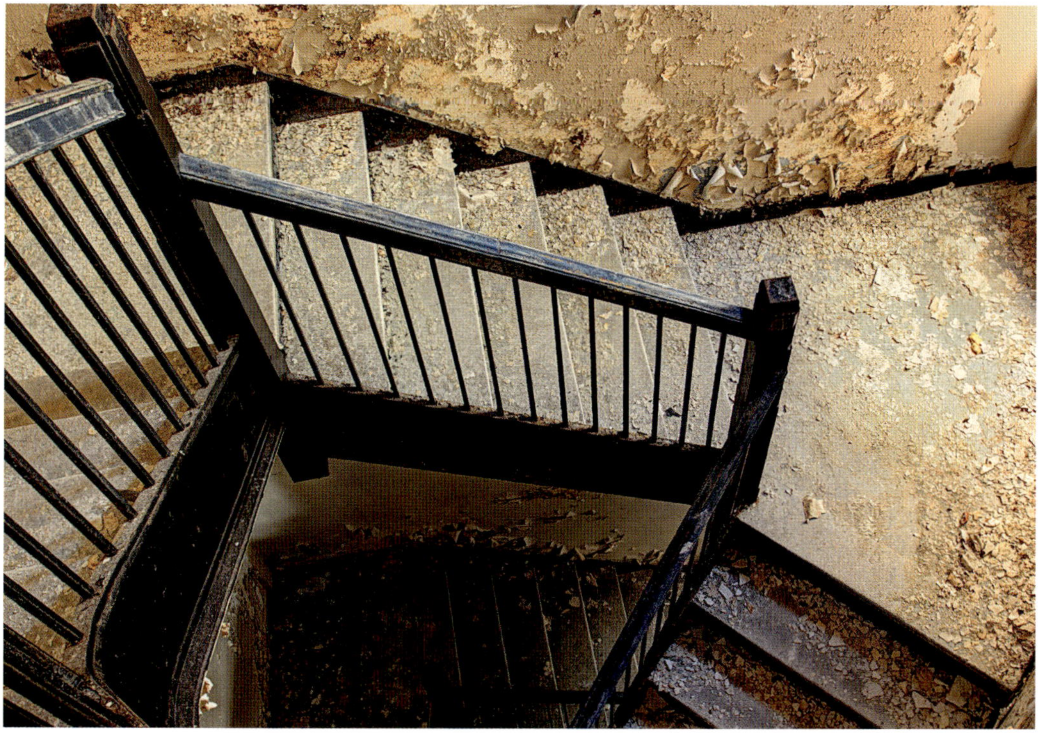

This triangular stairwell is situated off to the side of the arcade building.

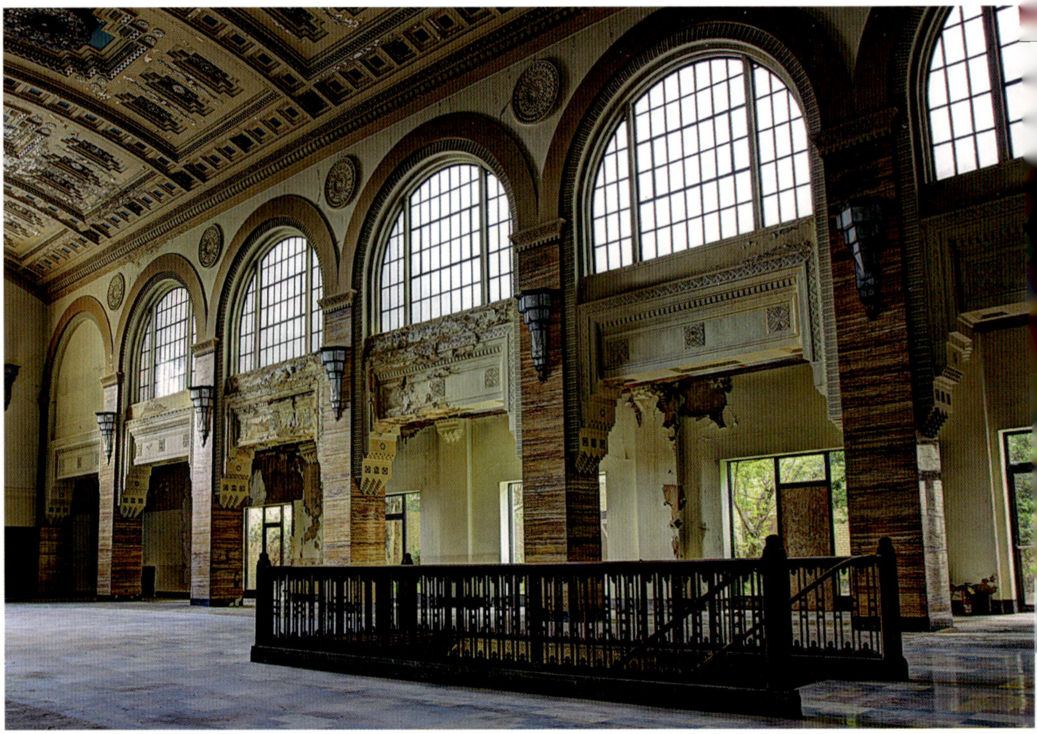

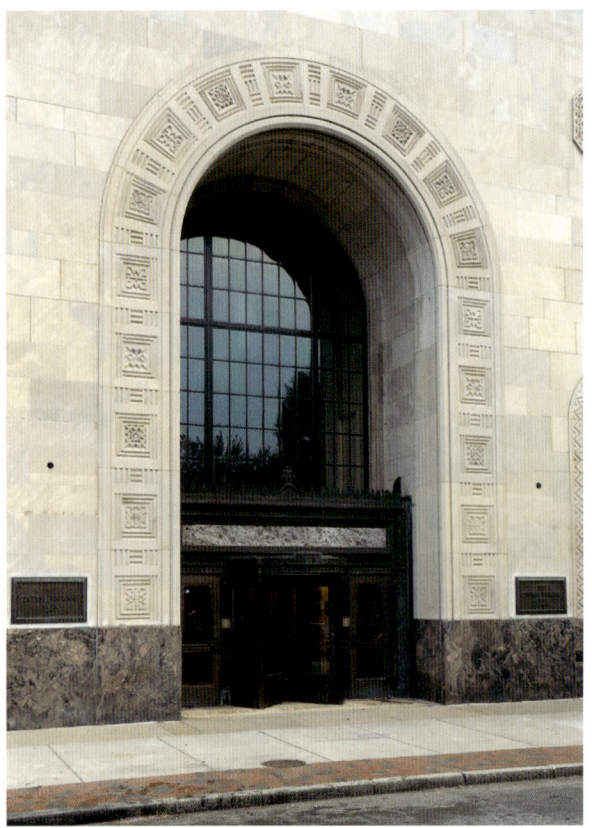

Left: Original entrance to Central National Bank, taken in 2019.

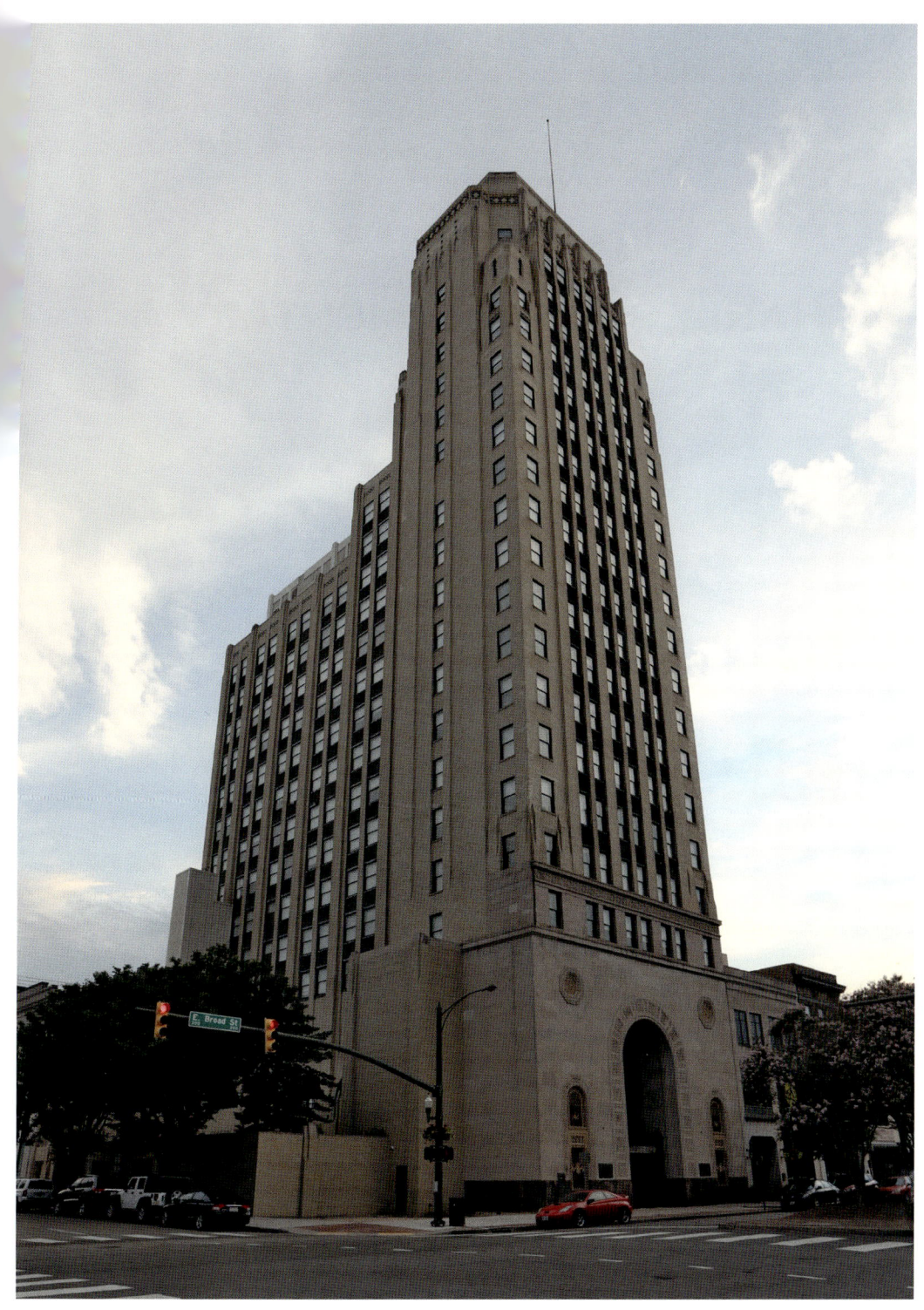

The renovated Deco at CNB Building in 2019.

10

CHARLES CITY ELEMENTARY

CHARLES CITY, VA

This former elementary school sits in a field, at the corner of two rural roads. There are a few houses nearby, but not much else is happening in this area. The construction type of this school is a rather traditional L-shaped brick building with a flat roof. The ceiling is relatively high, which is seen more commonly in the design of older schools.

Ivy vines were growing all around, up the walls, and in through some of the broken windows. There were several classrooms with ivy growing across interior walls as well. These sections of the vines contained no leaves, so they looked like tendrils that were slowly consuming the classrooms. A small cluster of bats had also made their home above one of the classrooms. I found a collection of them hanging in a section of the ceiling, seemingly unbothered by my presence.

It is difficult to confirm exactly how long this school has been vacant. The replacement Charles City Elementary School was constructed in 1993, located a few miles to the east, so it is likely that the old location ceased to operate as a school around the same time. I did find some newspapers inside the main office which were dated from 2001, so the property may have been used in some capacity after it closed down as a school. I am not optimistic about the future of this structure. It is unlikely that renovation would be worth the expense to a developer in such a rural location, and I suspect that this former school will continue to deteriorate until it is eventually destroyed.

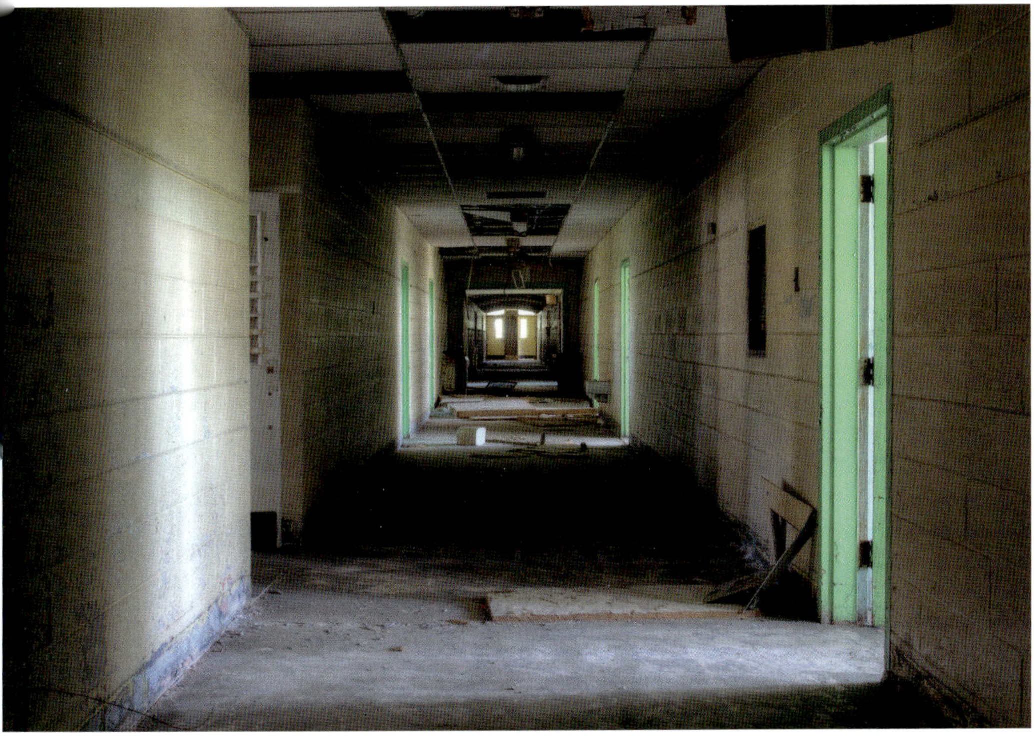

Above: Components hanging from the ceiling contributed to the eerie feeling inside this former school.

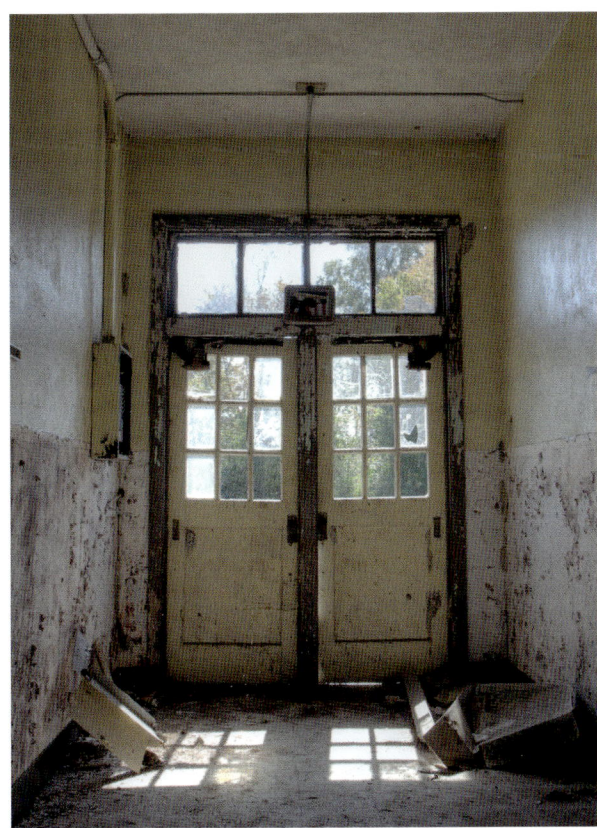

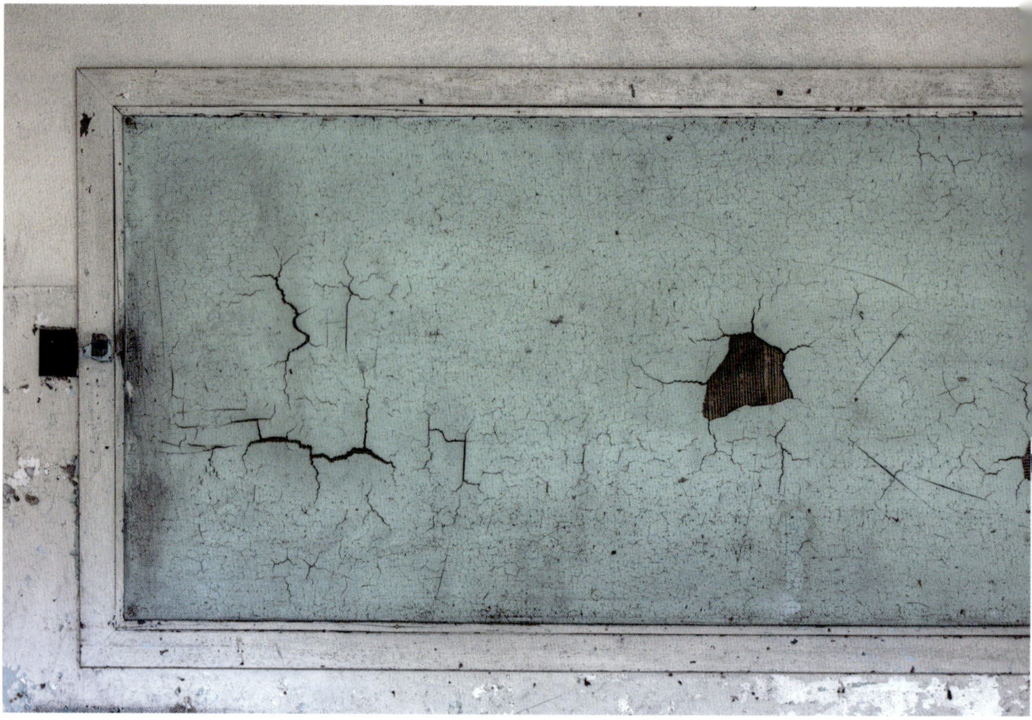

A former classroom chalkboard.

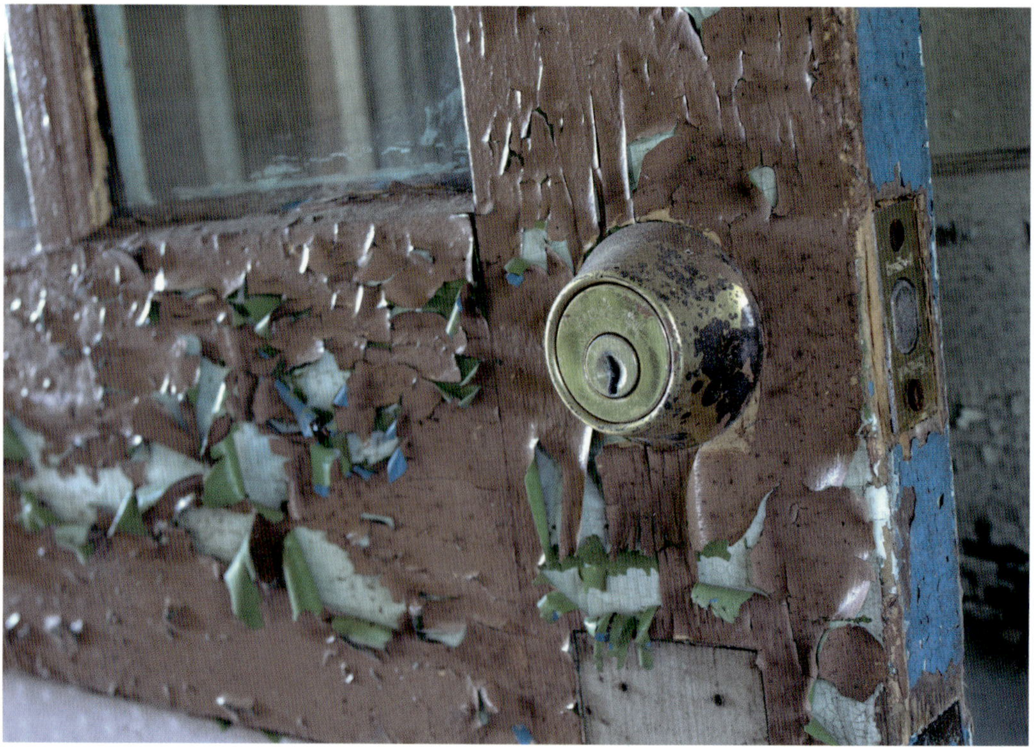

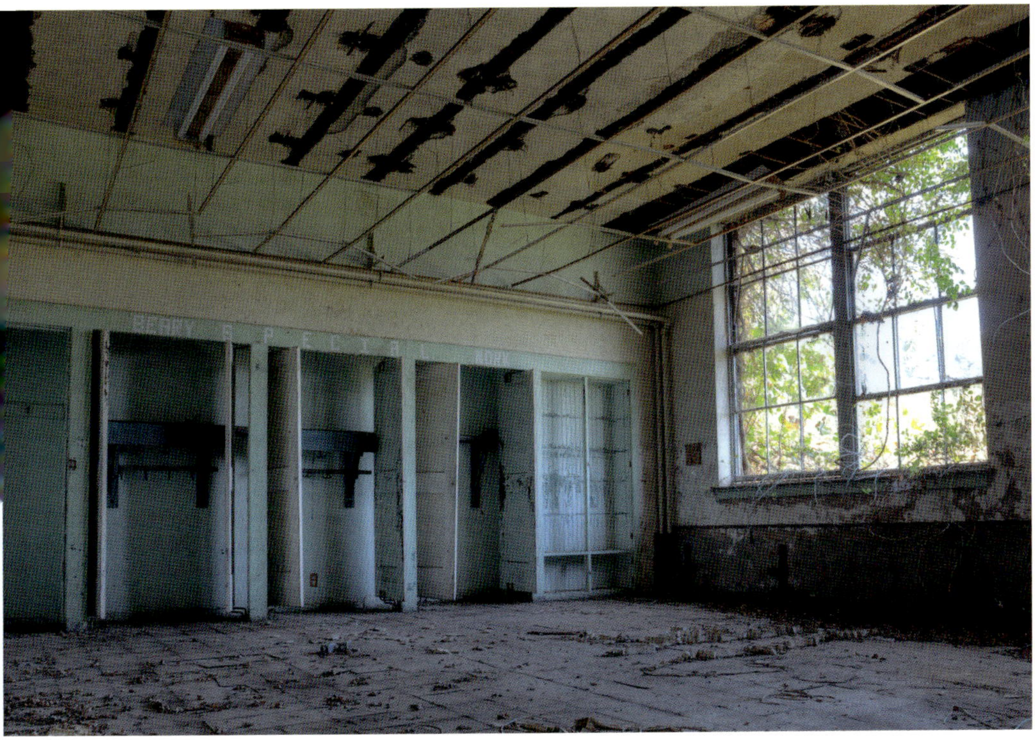

One of the former school classrooms.

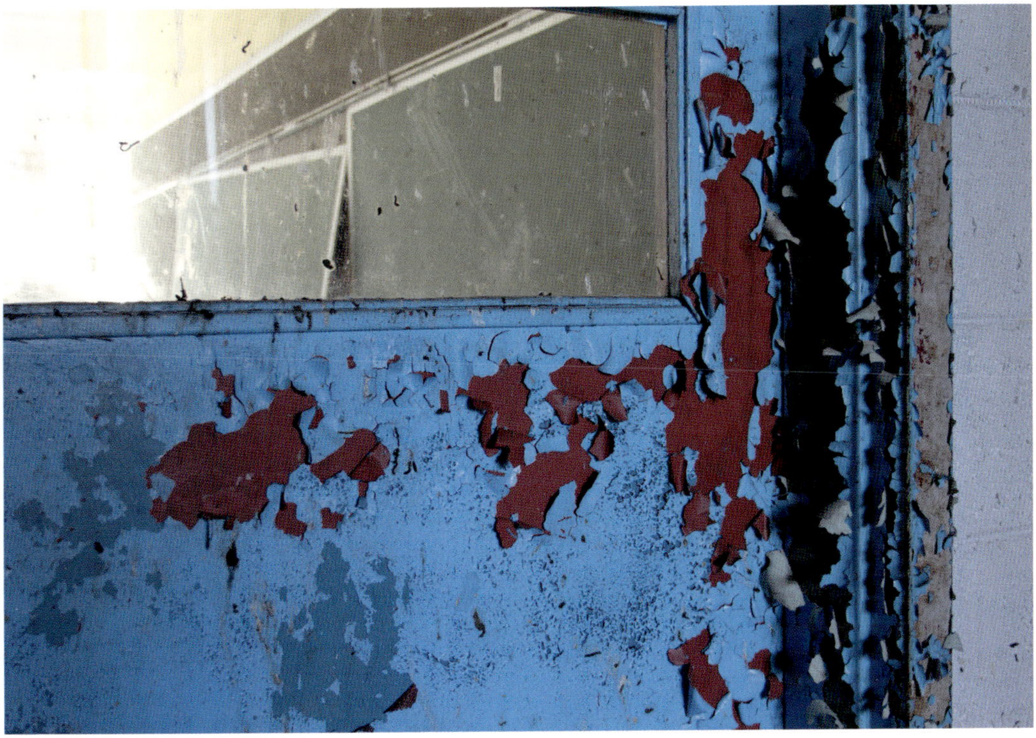

Peeling paint was a regular feature inside this school.

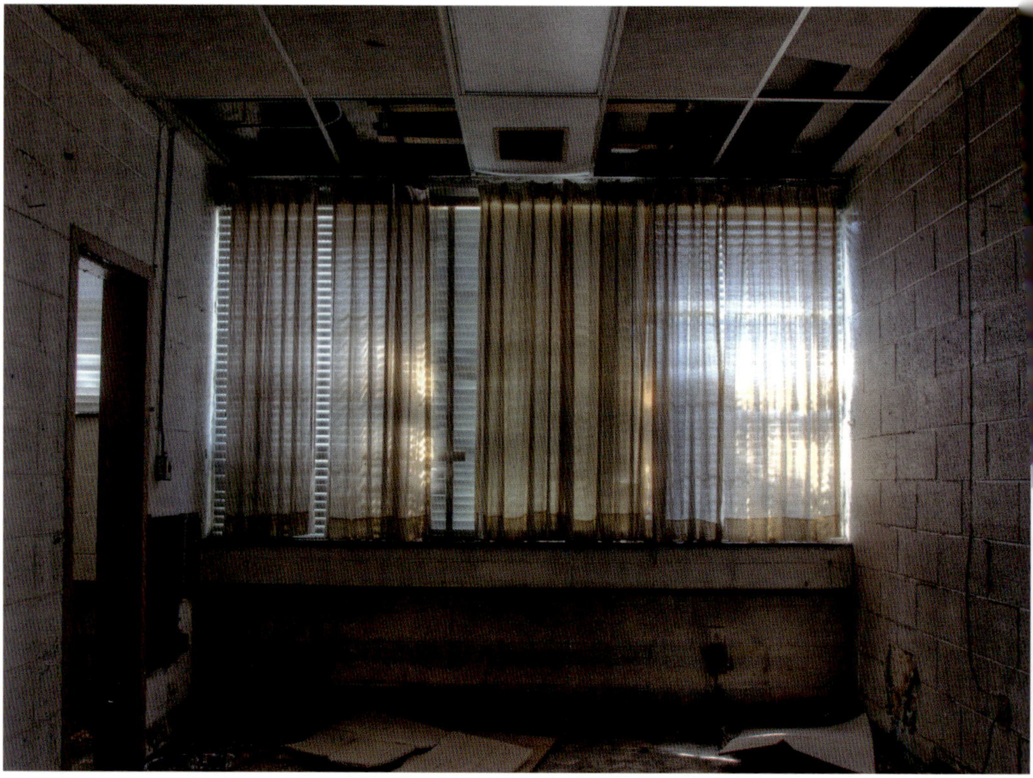

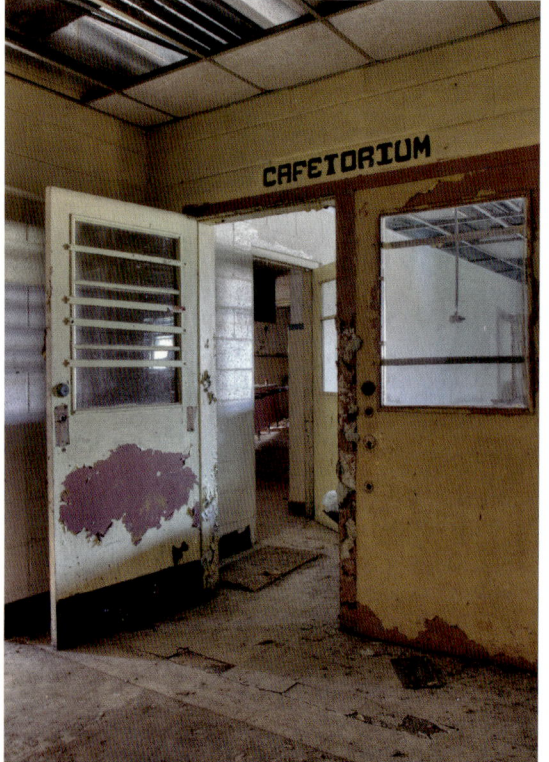

Above: Light comes through the curtains inside the school offices.

Left: This door leads to the kitchen and cafetorium.

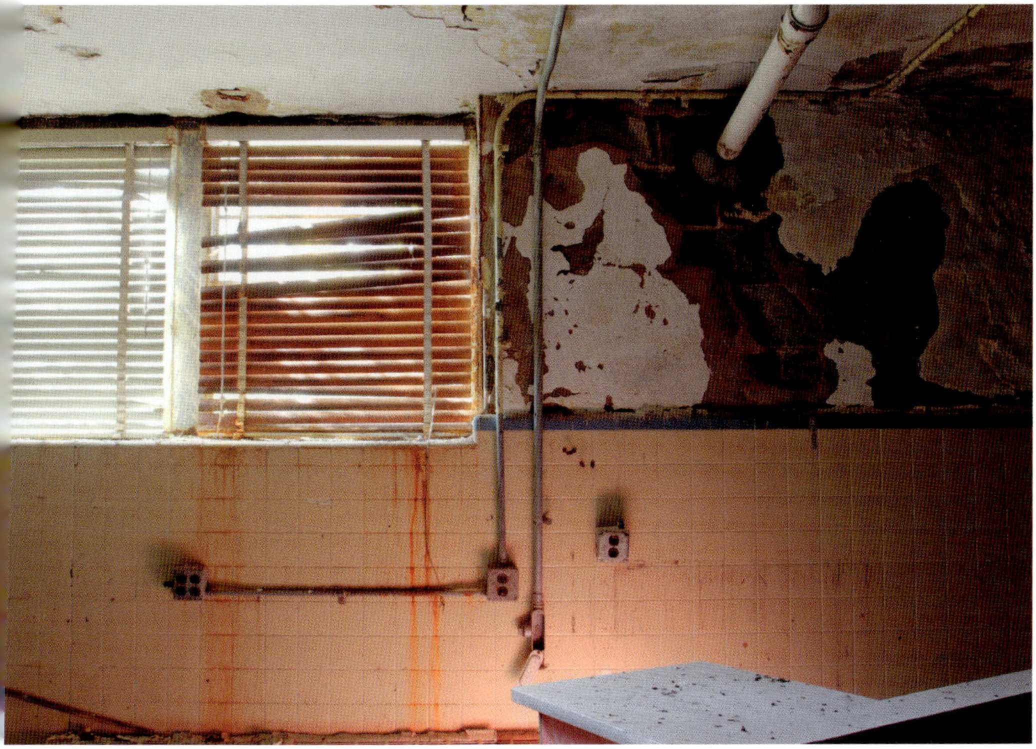

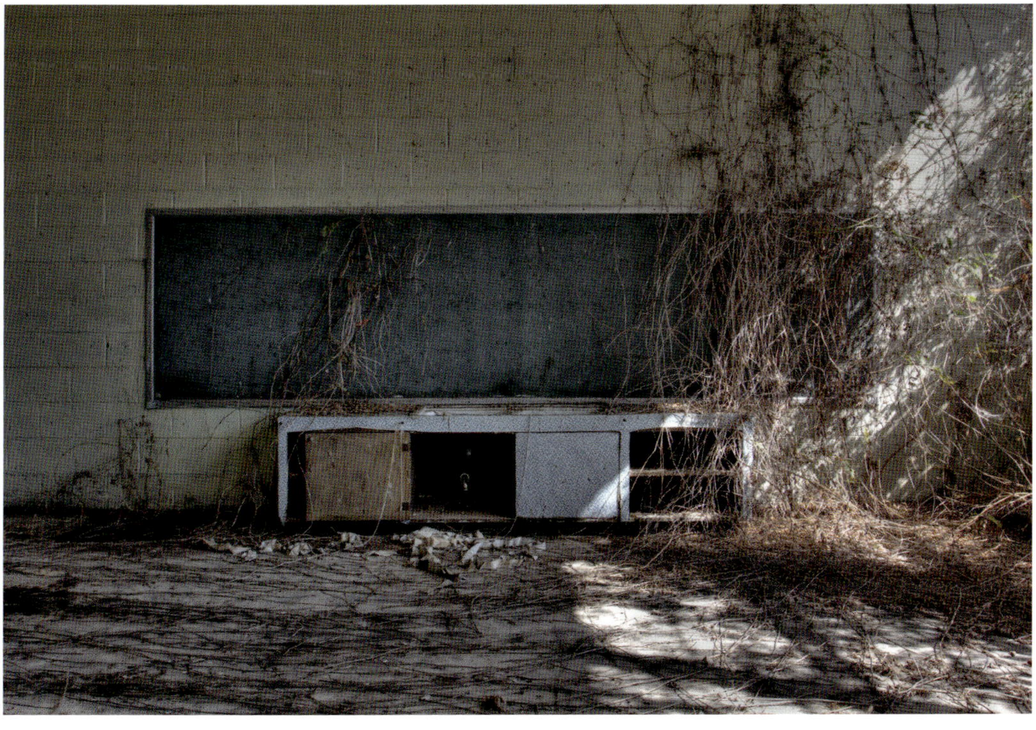

Ivy has come through the windows and started overtaking the classroom.

11

JARRATT SCHOOL

Jarratt, VA

This brick school building has an impressive two-story front entrance, featuring a pointed classical pediment atop five columns. The upper story appears to have functioned as the main floor, with an auditorium in the center of the layout, and smaller rooms on either side. The lower floor is partially underground, and it featured a kitchen, cafeteria, utility room, and a few other unidentified rooms.

Details are scarce regarding the prior use of the school, but it does appear to have been vacant for at least a few decades. This property is located behind an active funeral home, and a few of the rooms contained old mortuary equipment. There was also a collection of assorted items in the former auditorium, including a piano organ, upholstered chairs, a poster of a 1980s Chevrolet Caprice, and for some reason, a couple of couches that are standing on end. As with most abandoned schools, there was also a collection of old desks, chairs, and fading blackboards.

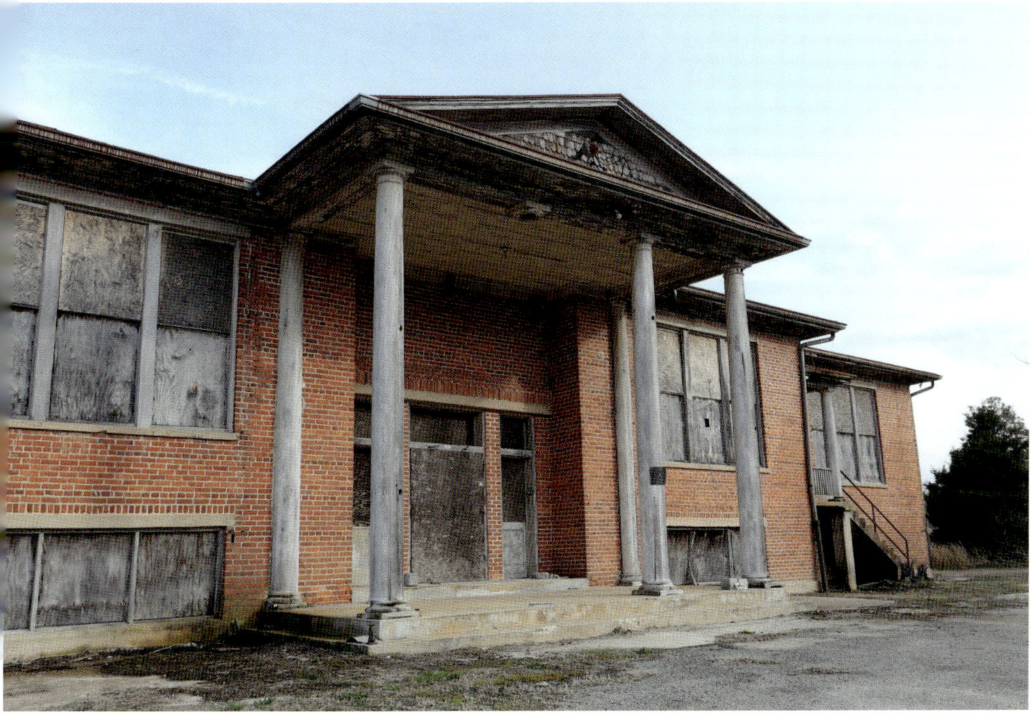

The two-story front entrance to this building is very imposing.

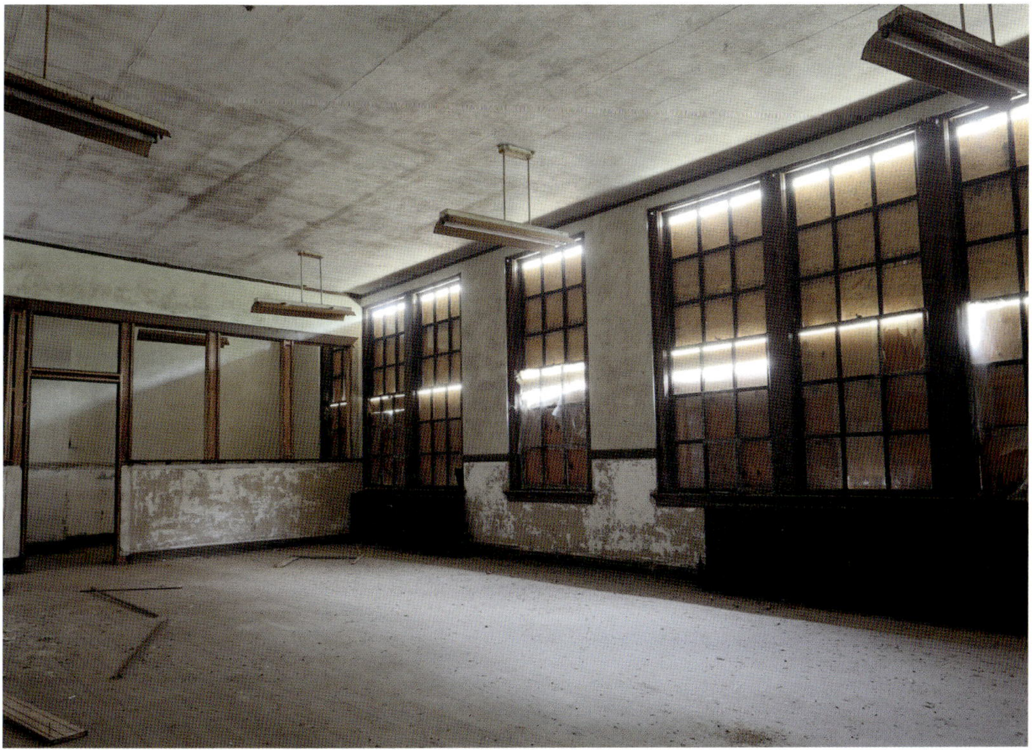

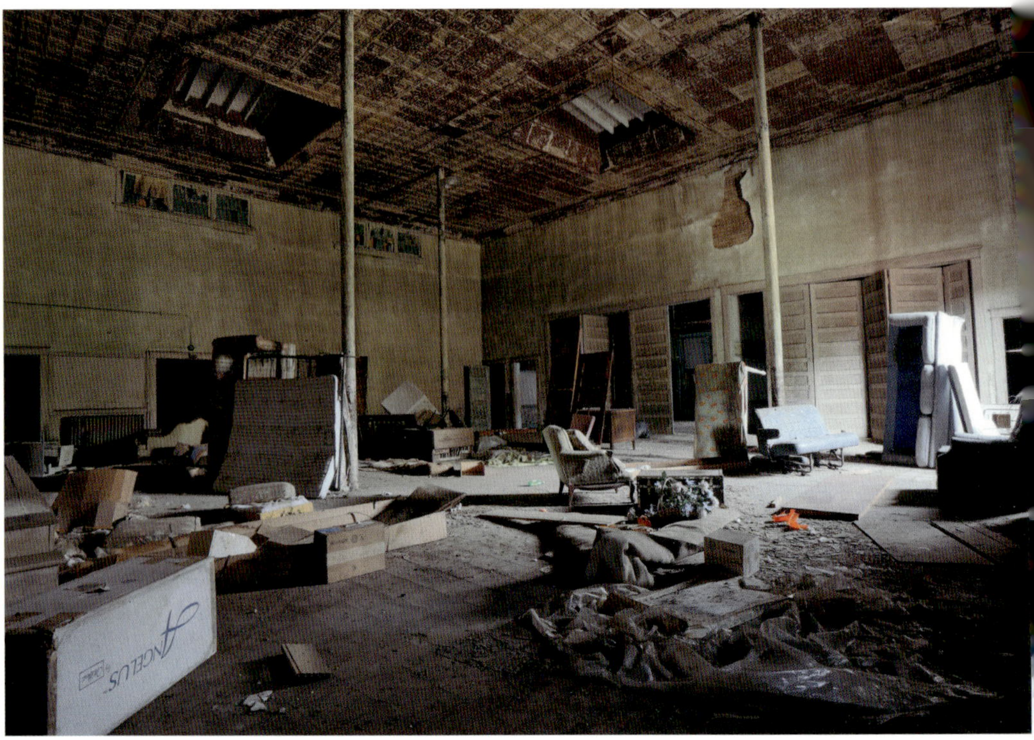

An assortment of decrepit household furniture.

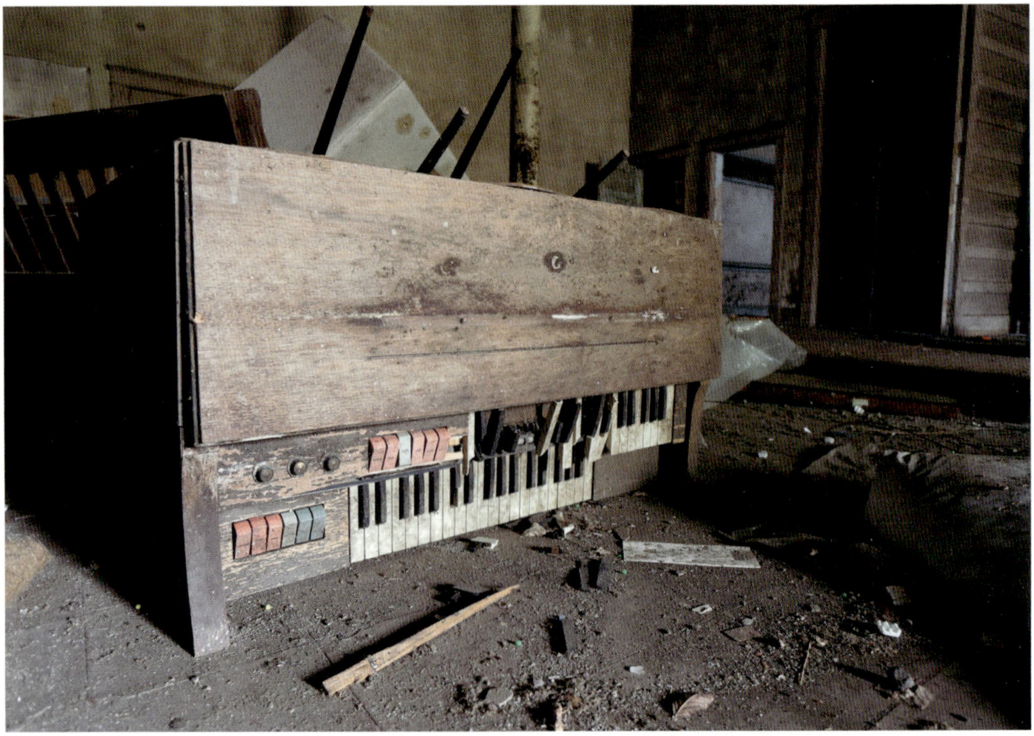

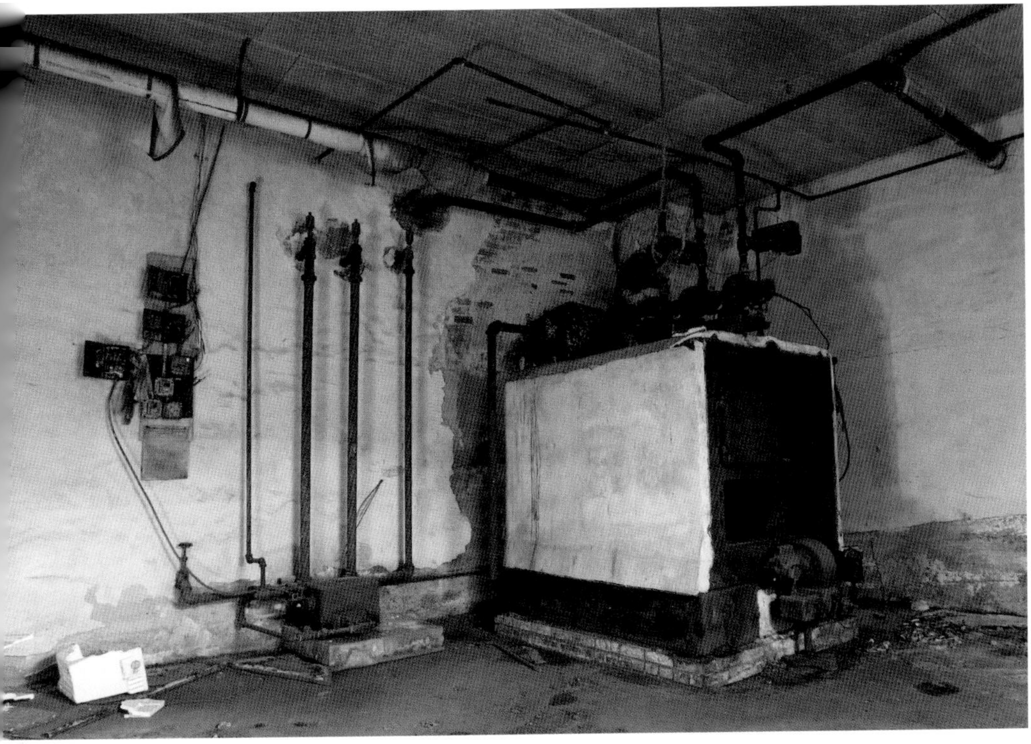

Inside the boiler room.

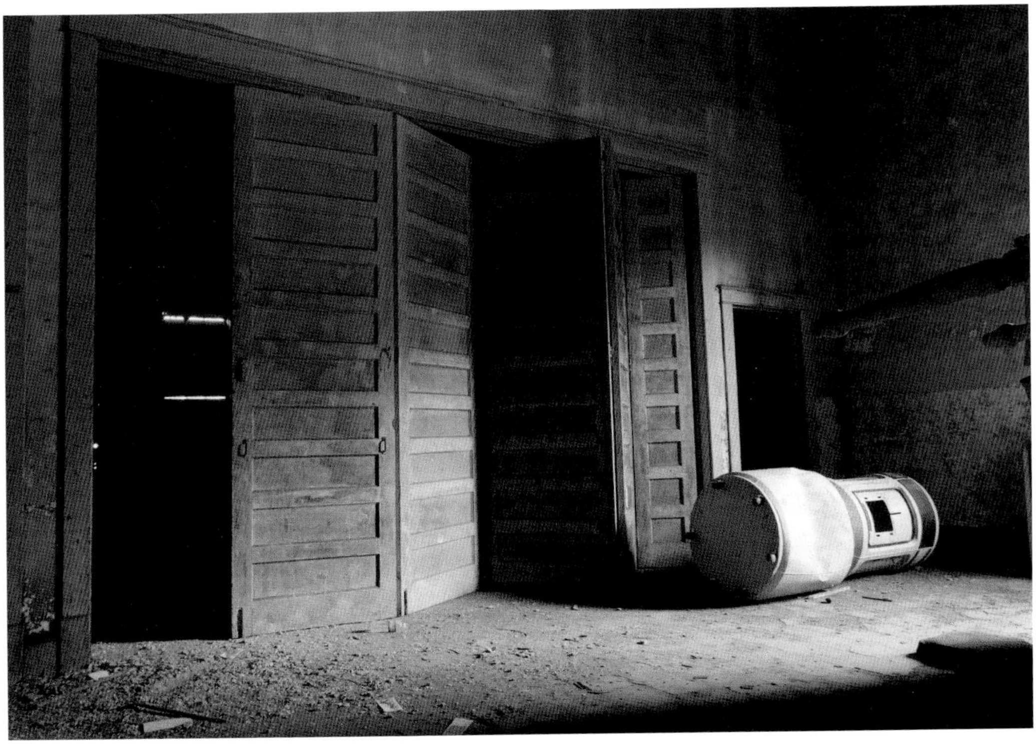

These are very tall doors; the door on the far right is a normal size interior door.

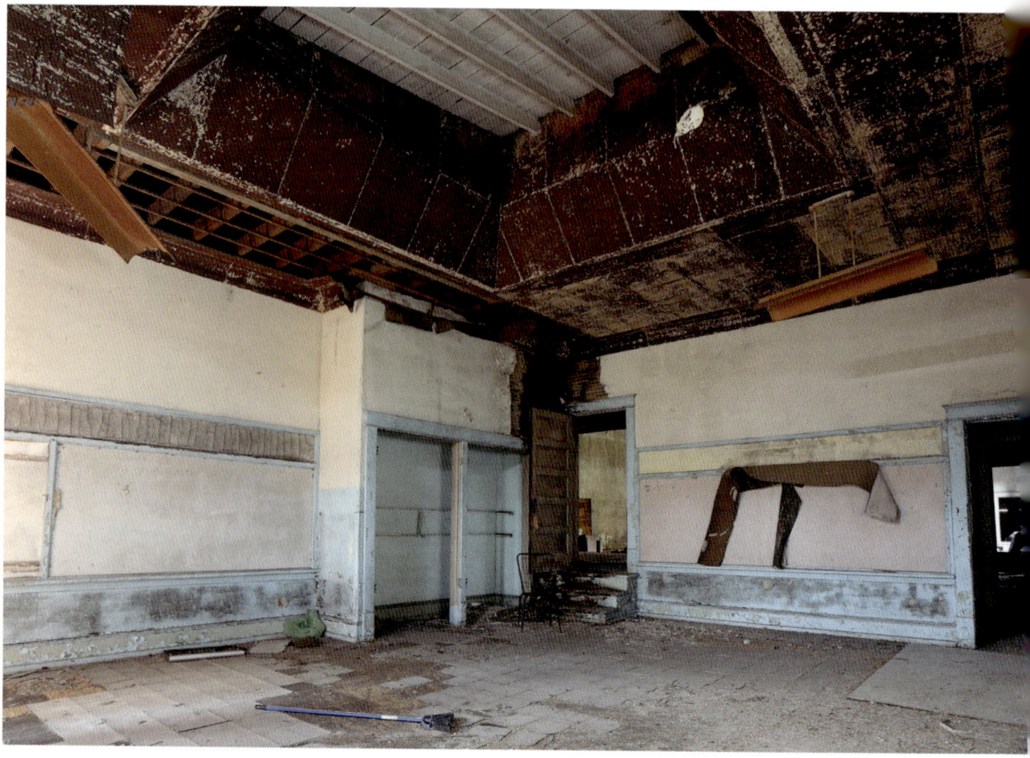

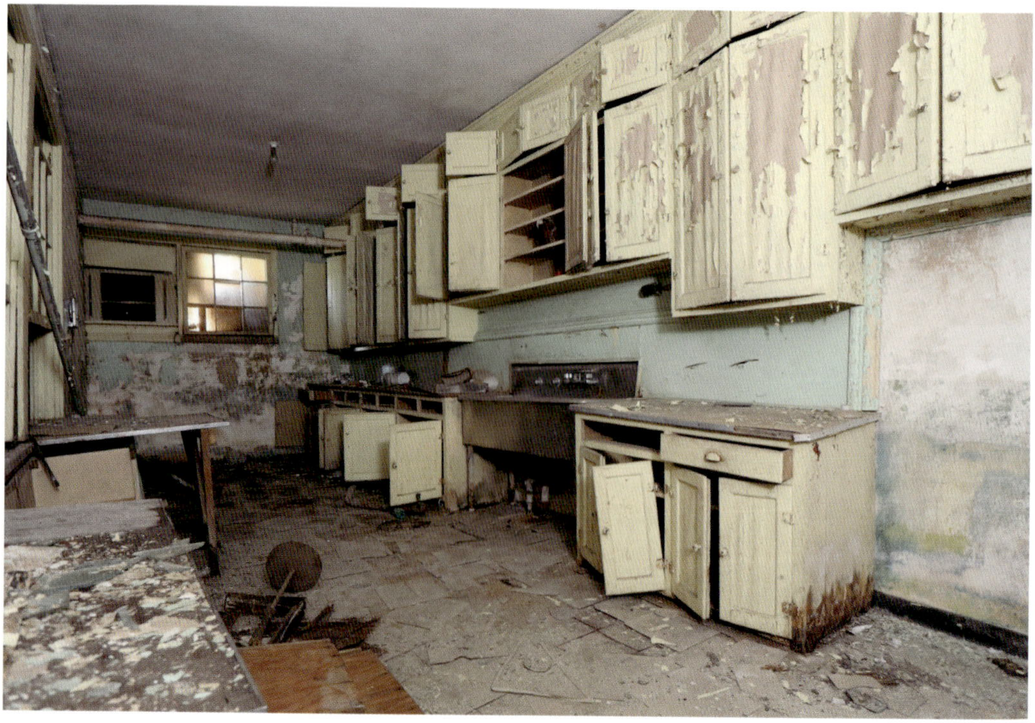

A kitchen down in the school basement.

12

HONEYWELL WAREHOUSE

HOPEWELL, VA

This industrial building in Hopewell was surrounded by cracked asphalt and several years' worth of tall grass. It appeared to have operated as a small production facility for protective helmets, possibly for military use. It is located just east of the city of Hopewell, on East Randolph Road. Though it appeared to be owned by Honeywell, an active chemical company with a manufacturing plant in the city of Hopewell, this particular building had not been used for many years.

The building was most likely first owned by Allied Signal, a chemical manufacturer that began operations in Hopewell in the 1940s. When Allied Signal purchased Honeywell in 1999, they elected to begin using the Honeywell name for the entire corporation. There were some items in this abandoned building with the Allied Signal name printed on them, while some others were branded as Honeywell. Based on some of the newspapers I found in the building, this facility likely ceased its operations a couple of years after the merger between the two companies.[1]

Most of the materials in this building appeared to be related to protective helmets, particularly the unfinished helmet shells that were littered about in several rooms. However, there were other items that did particularly not make sense, such as a table full of clothing buttons, and a closet with old sports trophies. There was also a section of offices with collapsed walls and heavy damages to the roof. This is a fairly simple but robust concrete building, and it will be interesting to see if Honeywell chooses to revitalize, demolish, or continue ignoring this facility.

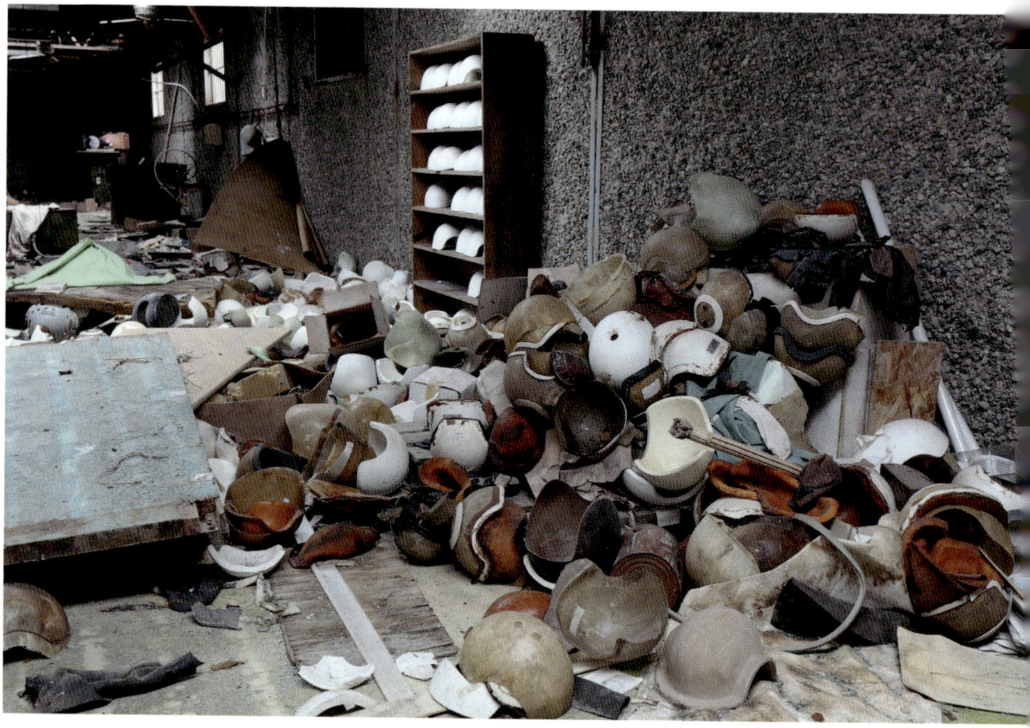

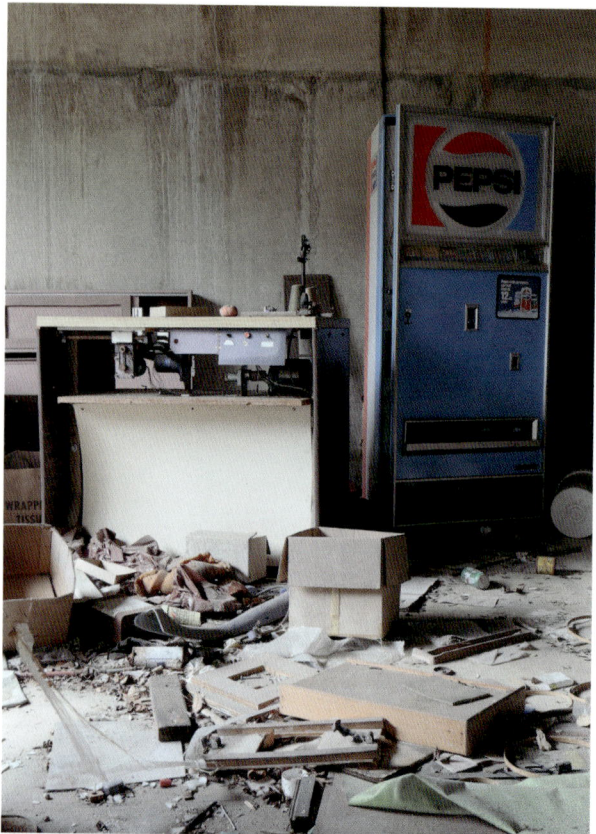

Above: Multifarious assortment of helmets.

Left: Retro soda machine inside the warehouse.

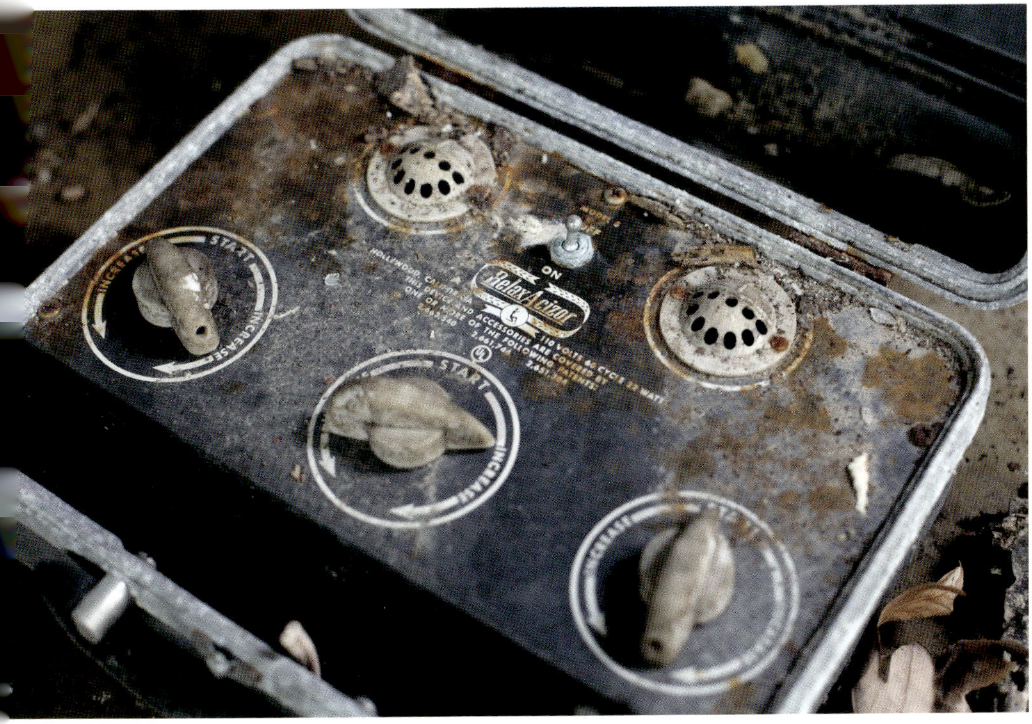

A weight loss device from the 1950s that was considered so dangerous that it was banned in the United States.

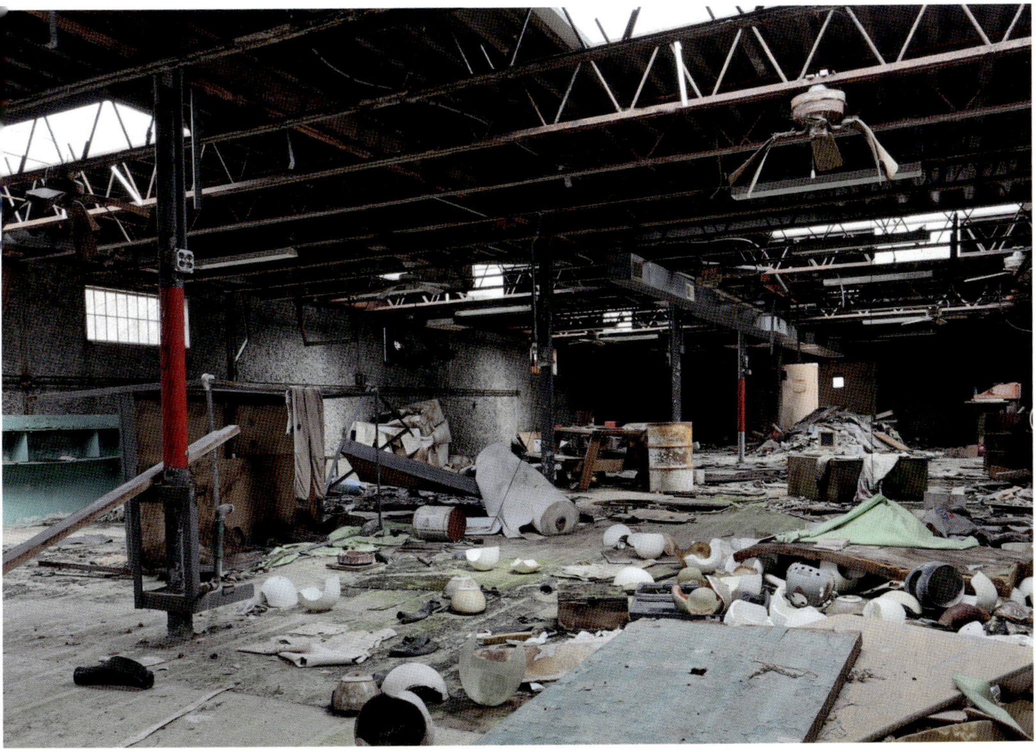

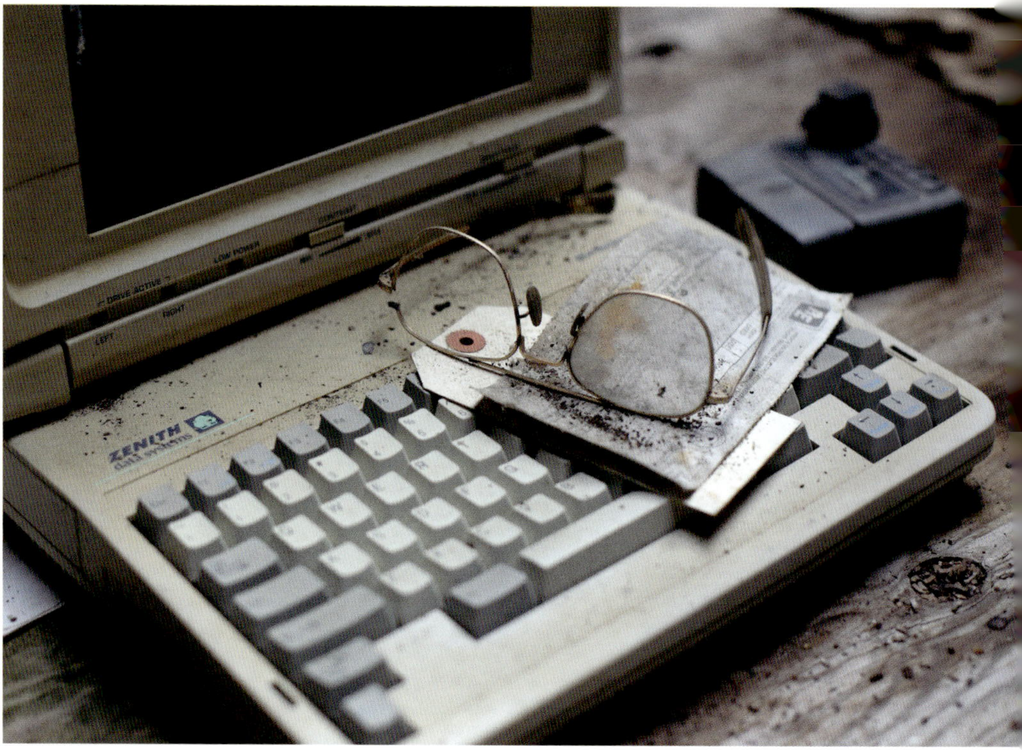

1980s laptop computer complete with 1980s glasses.

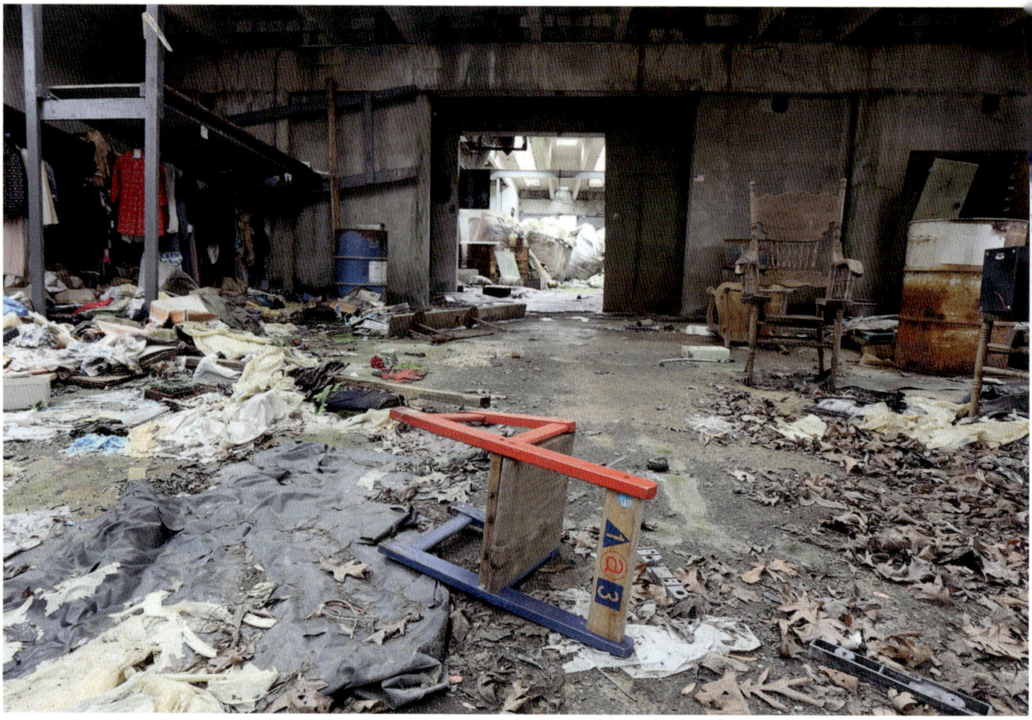

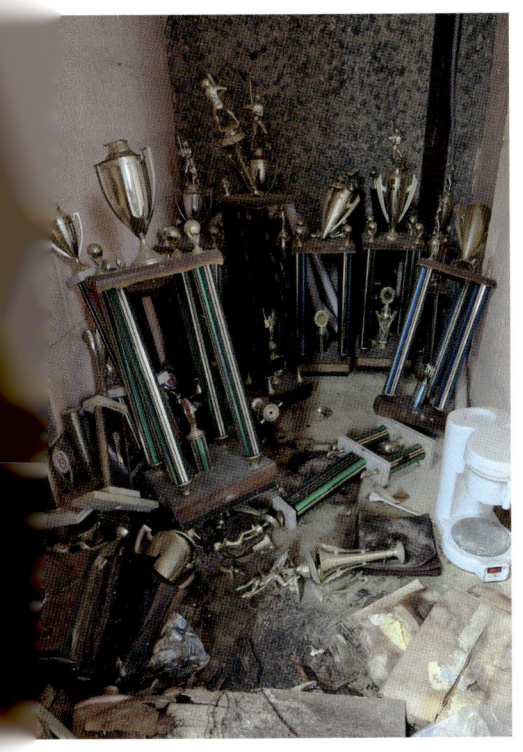

Small closet full of unfinished trophies.

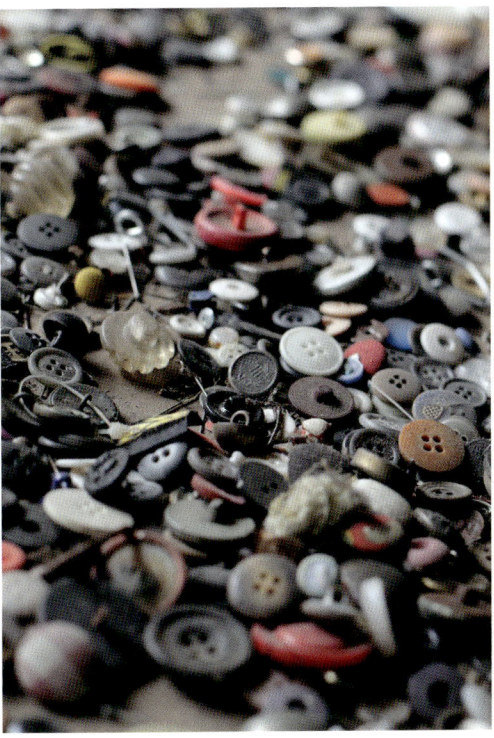

There was a large tabletop covered in loose buttons.

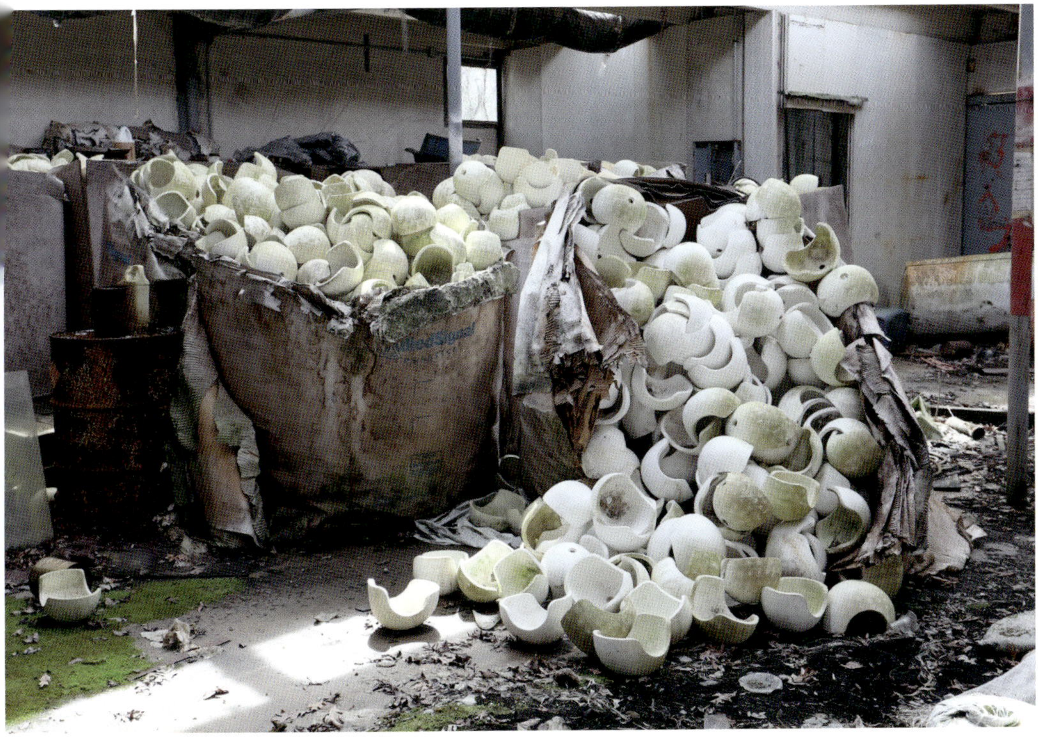

Originally these were new helmet shells, but now they are spilling out of their water-damaged cardboard boxes.

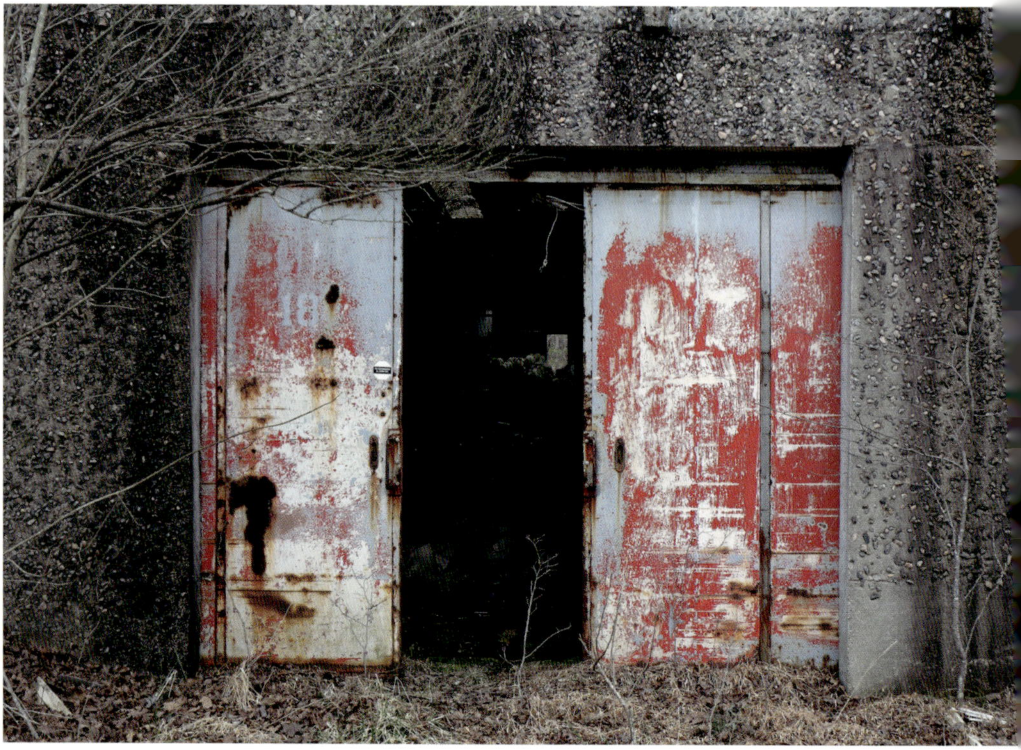

One of the exterior doors on this warehouse.

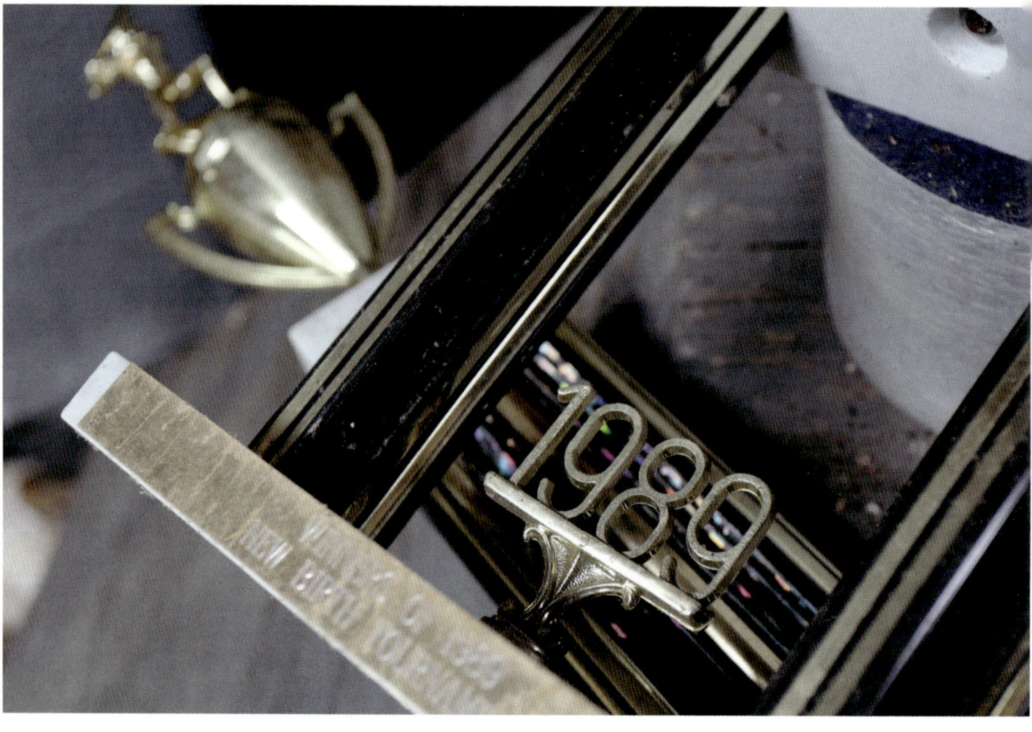

This is one of the sports trophies left behind.

13

UNION LEVEL GHOST TOWN

SOUTH HILL, VA

The most striking thing about the remains of Union Level is the remoteness of this area. Located a few miles west of South Hill, and surrounded by farms, I discovered this collection of dilapidated buildings. They were so close to one another that there is barely room to walk between them. It looked as though this arrangement of buildings was plucked from a busy nineteenth-century American city, and then deposited out here in the country.

Union Level was established in the 1840s, and served as a way station for those travelling by wagon. There was a railway depot in the town, and it could be used by passengers who wished to travel by train. This small town was once surrounded by tobacco farms. The town suffered some decline in the late nineteenth century, in the wake of the Civil War. However, this was still an active small town in the early twentieth century. There were as many as twenty businesses in Union Level at that time, including barber shops, a bank, general stores, a pharmacy, and auto service garages. However, the town deteriorated somewhat further in the midst of the Great Depression. This brought about the closure of several businesses, including the bank. The drugstore and two general stores closed down in the 1970s, and the train depot was demolished in 1980. Several buildings must have been torn down over the course of the twentieth century, because these six buildings are nearly all that is left. These remaining buildings were occupied by some of the aforementioned businesses, including the bank, a general store, and a boarding house.[1]

As I explored these properties, I discovered that most of these buildings were being used for storage of some sort. Products from past decades were everywhere: a Kenmore wringer washer from the 1940s; an Underwood No. 5 typewriter, likely manufactured sometime between 1910-1930; and an unsettling amount of bird feathers.

One of the stores was suffering from a completely collapsed second floor, and also a missing a roof. There were disintegrating floorboards, buckled walls, and one severely warped front porch. It would take a lot of work to restore these buildings. Sadly, this property may fall into an impasse suffered by many rural abandoned buildings. If the land is worth less than the cost of demolition, then the buildings will not be destroyed or renovated anytime soon. If they remain untouched, these buildings will continue being taken over by nature, one decade at a time.

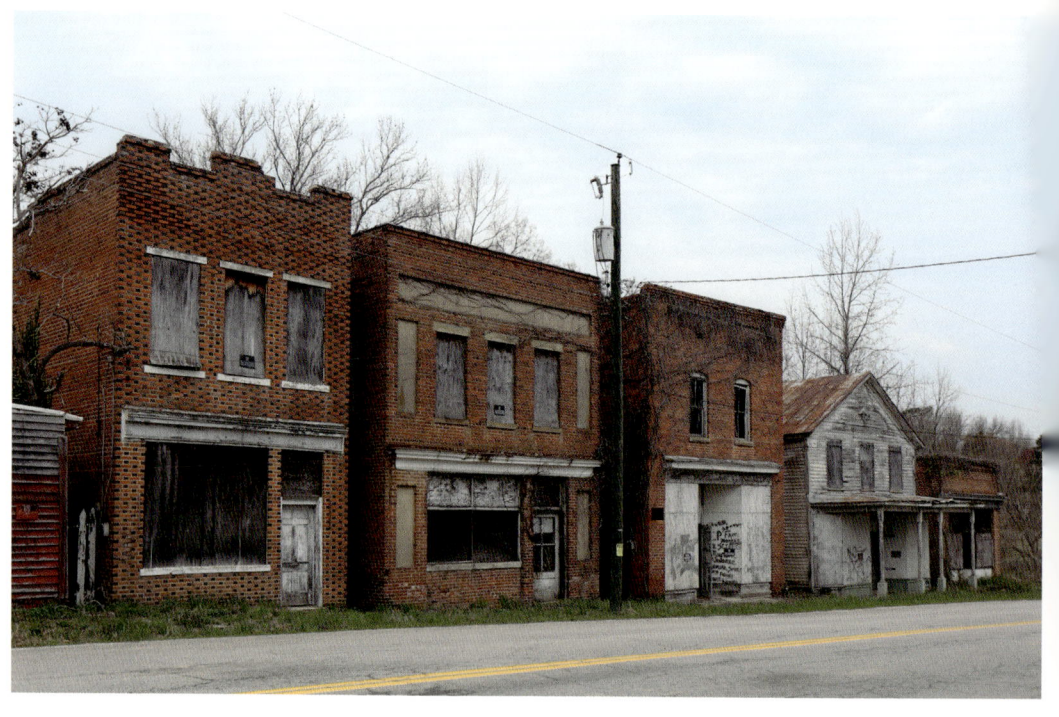

It is hard to tell from this one photo, but this block of buildings is surrounded on either side with farmland.

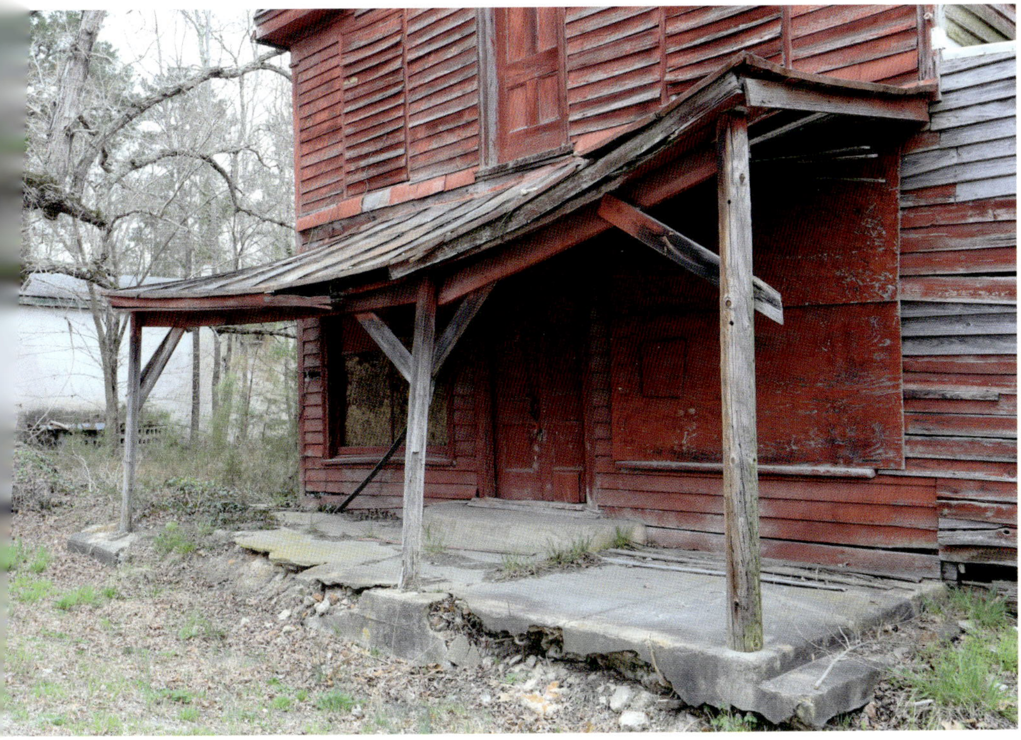

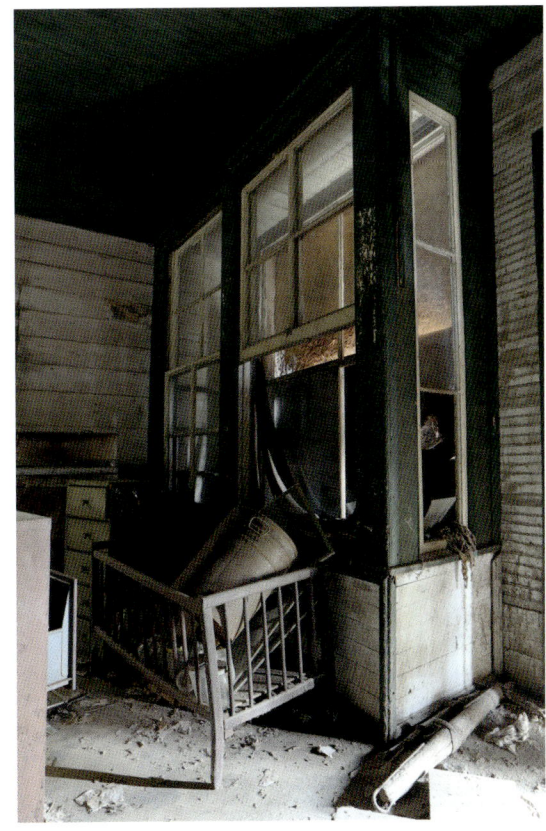

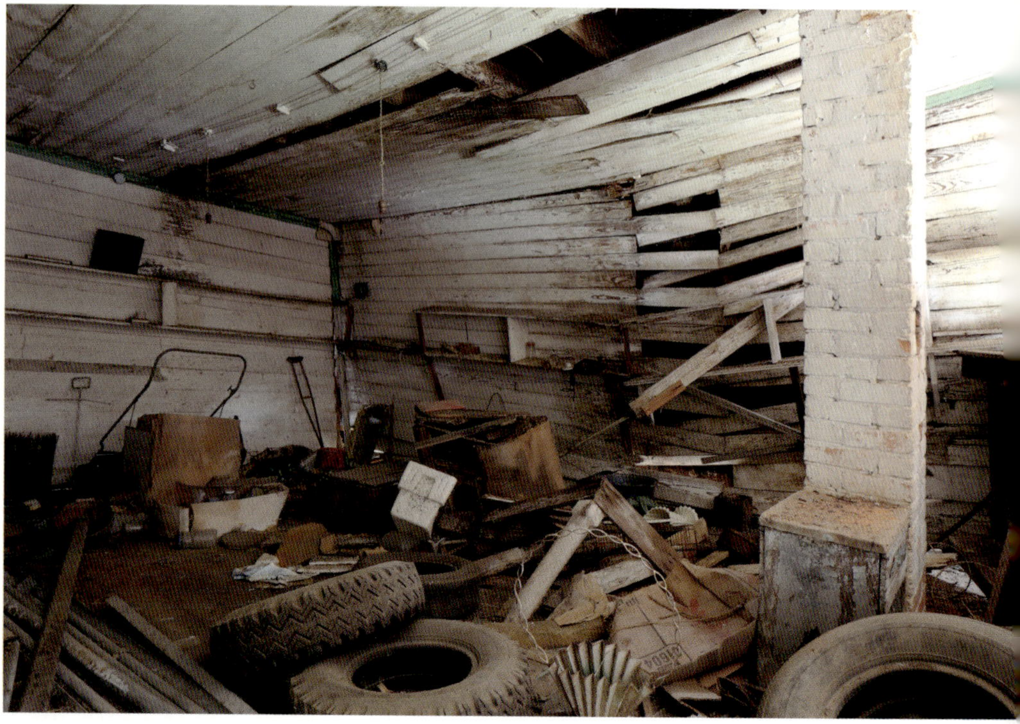

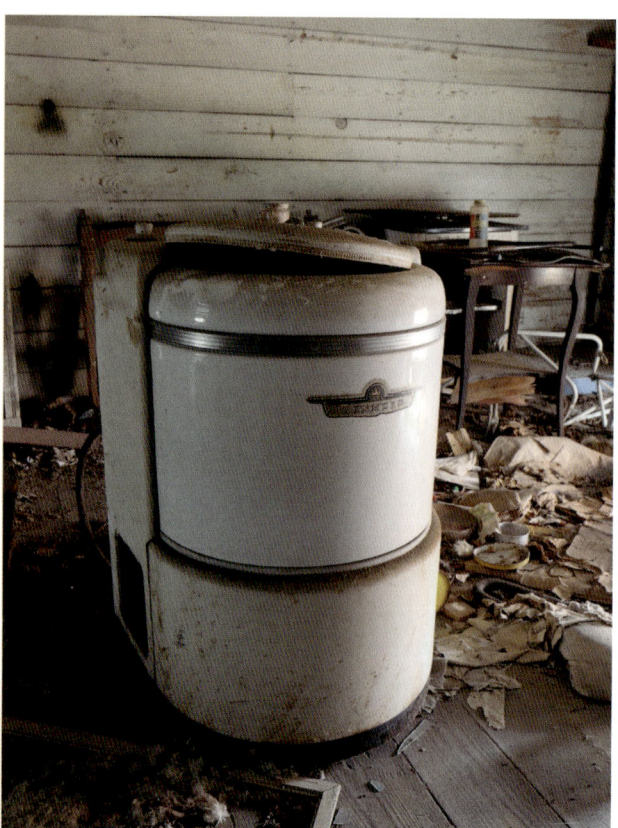

Above: The slow collapse of this building has bowed the ceiling and the walls.

Left: A Kenmore wringer washer from the 1940s.

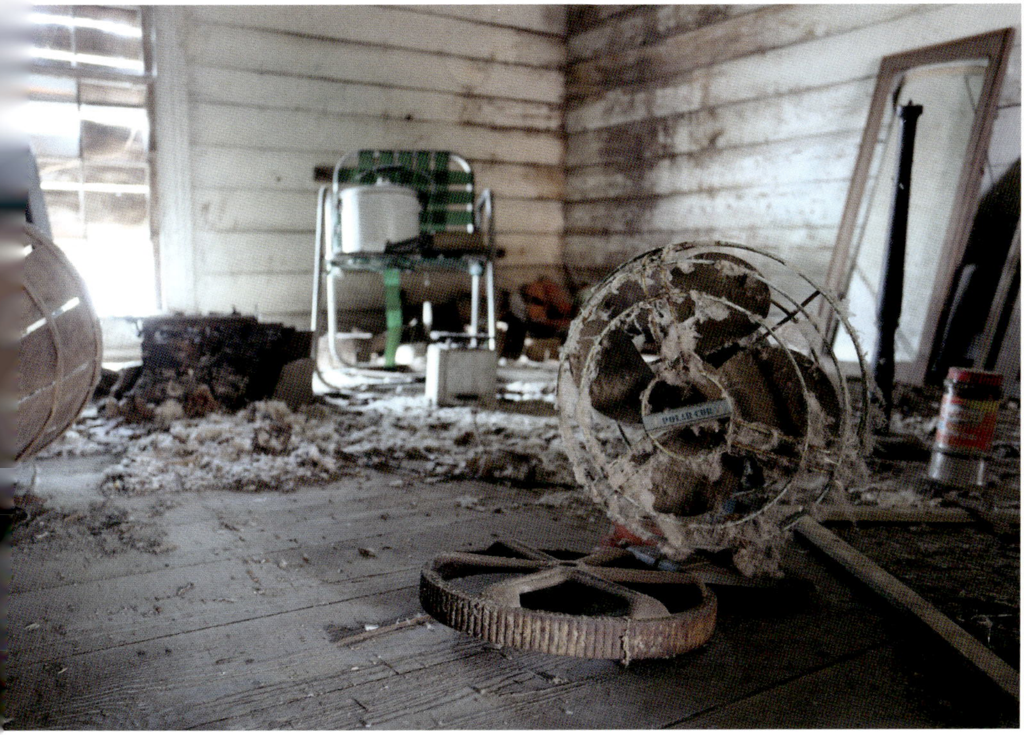

Some assorted items in a building attic.

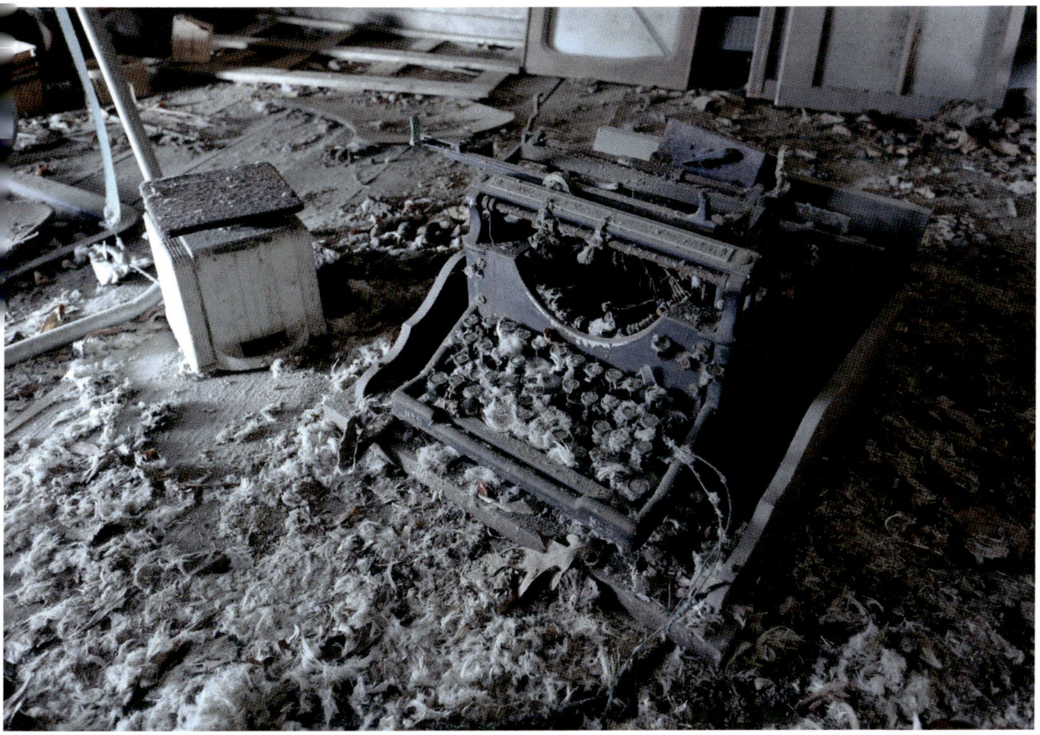

A typewriter covered in dust and feathers.

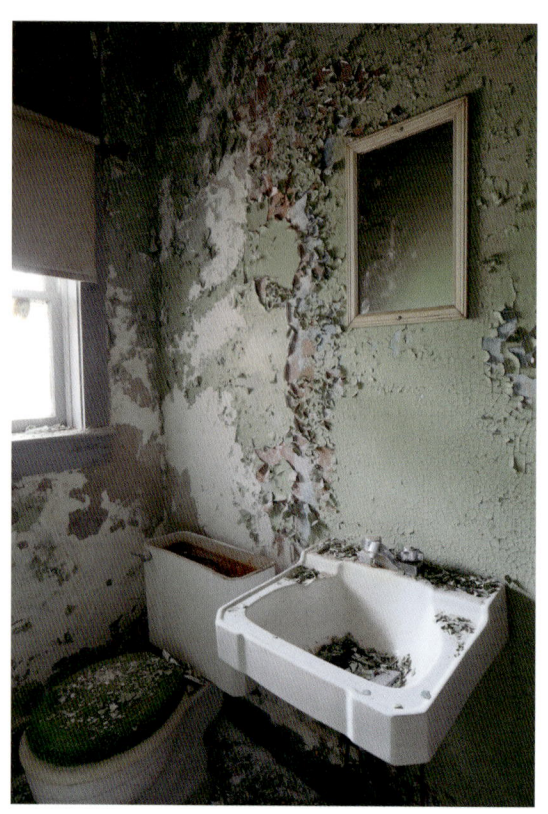

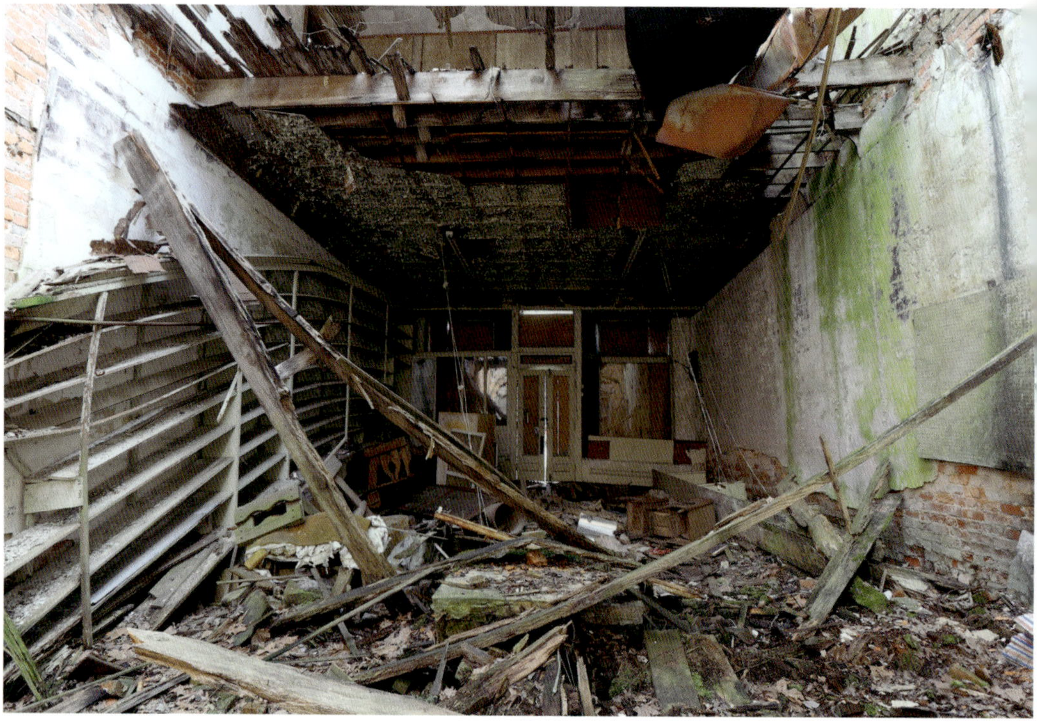

Dilapidated shelves and structural damage inside this former store.

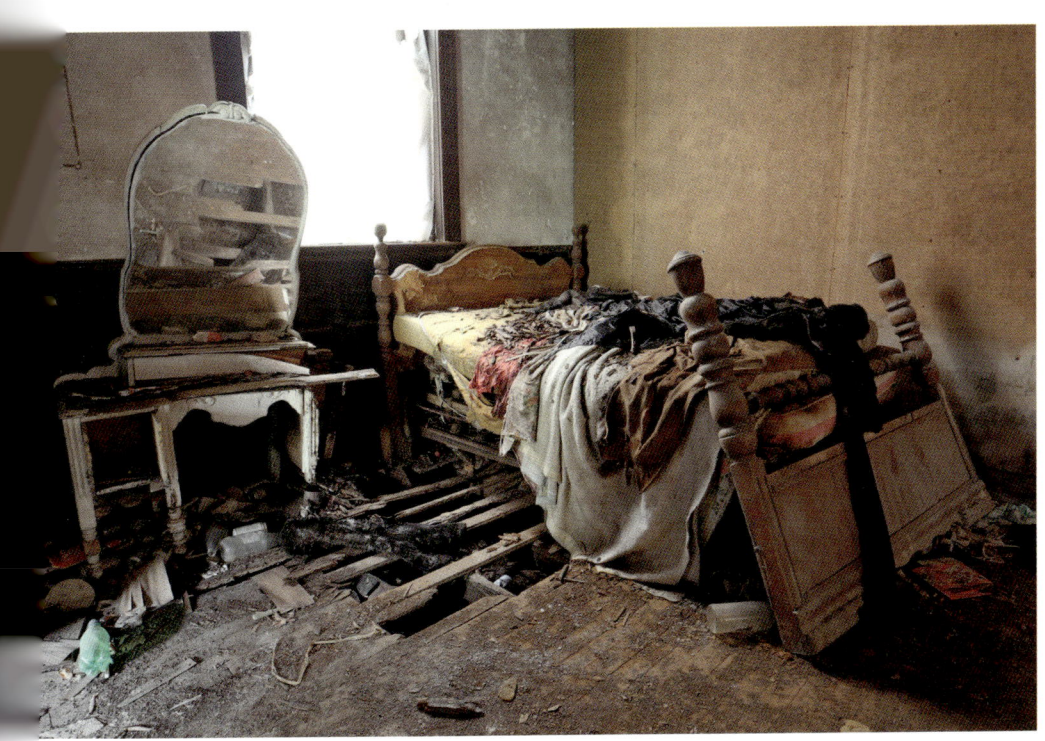

This bed looks like it is about to fall through the floor.

Endnotes

St Francis de Sales School

1. Arnold, C. M., "St. Francis DeSales School," *Virginia Department of Historic Resources Preliminary Information Form* (Community Housing Partners, 2002), p.7-8.
2. Palmore, M., "The Castle on the James," *Powhatan Today*, December 13, 1990.
3. Arnold, op. cit., p. 7-8.
4. Ibid.
5. Lazarus, J. M., "Nonprofit's effort to buy St. Emma-St. Francis property collapses", *Richmond Free Press*, October 4, 2018.

C&O Freight Receiving Depot

1. Jacobe, S., and Wiggs, L., "C&O Freight Receiving Depot," *Virginia Department of Historic Resources Architectural Survey Form* (Virginia Department of Historic Resources, 2018), p. 1-3.
2. Ibid.

Federated Paper Board Company Mill

1. Langan, J. V., and Holma, M., and Staton, H. D., and Kraus, N., "Standard Paper Company," *Virginia Department of Historic Resources Architectural Survey Form* (Virginia Department of Historic Resources, 2019), p. 1-4.
2. Ibid.
3. Ibid.

VIRGINIA RENAISSANCE FAIRE

1. Karalee, D., "Renaissance Faire, VA," *Lucent Moments,* 31 March 2009. Web. 22 May 2019.
2. Ibid.
3. Ibid.
4. Lucia, "Abandoned: The Failure of the Virginia Renaissance Faire, Fredericksburg," *The Ghost in My Machine,* 26 November 2018. Web. 29 June 2019.
5. Ibid.
6. Karalee, op. cit.

SOUTHERN BISCUIT COMPANY

1. Author Unknown, "Southern Biscuit Company," *Virginia Department of Historic Resources PIF Resource Information Sheet* (Virginia Department of Historic Resources, 2011), p. 2-7.
2. Ibid.
3. Ibid.
4. Ibid.
5. Ames, A., "The Last FFVs," *Virginia Living,* October 2005, p. 72-73.

FULTON GAS WORKS

1. Author Unknown, "Fulton Gas Works," *Virginia Department of Historic Resources Intensive Level Survey* (Virginia Department of Historic Resources, 2007), p. 1-4.
2. Slipek, E., "The Ruins of Richmond," *Style Weekly,* 12 July 2016. Web. 22 May 2019.
3. Author Unknown, op. cit., p. 1-4.
4. Kollatz Jr., H., "Dreaming of Green," *Richmond Magazine,* 1 May 2004. Web. 22 May 2019.

CENTRAL NATIONAL BANK

1. Campbell, D. L., "The CNB Way: A Brief History of the Bank," Public Relations Pamphlet (Central National Bank, 1978), p. 2-6.
2. Ibid.
3. Author Unknown, "The Central National Bank Building," Public Relations Pamphlet (Central National Bank, April 1977), p. 1-6.
4. Author Unknown, "Central Fidelity Bank, N.A.," *Virginia Department of Historic Resources Reconnaissance Level Survey* (Virginia Department of Historic Resources, 2010), p. 1-3.
5. Watson, P., "Wachovia Branches Once Central Fidelity," *Daily Press,* 22 April 2001. Web. 23 May 2019.

HONEYWELL WAREHOUSE

1. Deutsch, C. H., and Holson, L. M., "Allied Signal and Honeywell to Announce Merger Today," *New York Times,* 7 June 1999. Web. 22 May 2019.

UNION LEVEL GHOST TOWN

1. Bowers, M., "Before Union Level Was a Ghost Town!! 1940," *The Old House Life,* 31 May 2018. Web. 22 May 2019.